ROBERTO ROSSELLINI

series edited and designed by Ian Cameron

ROBERTO ROSSELLINI

José Luis Guarner
translated by
Elisabeth Cameron

Praeger

BOOKS THAT MATTER

Published in the United States of America in 1970
by Praeger Publishers, Inc.
111 Fourth Avenue, New York, N.Y. 10003

Library of Congress Catalog Card Number:
77-99497

Produced by November Books Limited

Printed in Great Britain

The author wishes to thank Leonardo Fioravanti,
Director of the Centro Sperimentale di Cinemato-
grafia, whose kindness in making available for
study films preserved in the Cineteca Nazionale
(Rome) has made this work possible, as also has
that of Fausto Montesanti and Guido Cincotti.
The help of José de las Casas and José Fernández-
Cormenzana (TVE), Henri Langlois (Cinémathèque Française), Paola Cortese (Rai),
Arnaldo Giusti (Dino De Laurentiis Cine-
matografica) and Salvatore Riggi (ARCI) has
also been valuable.

Thanks are also due to Hélène Girard for help
in editing the original text in French, and to
Néstor Almendros, Edoardo Bruno, Vittorio
Cottafavi, Judith Ginsberg, Jorge Grau, Román
Gubern, Lambros Liaropoulos, Marcella Mariani,
José María Otero, Juan Manuel Otero, Maurizio
Ponzi, Renzo Rossellini Jr, Abdy Shama-Levi,
Piero Zanotto and the Biblioteca del Cinema
'Delmiro de Caralt'.

Stills by courtesy of Cineteca Nazionale,
Fotogramas, Film Ideal, Orizzonte 2000,
National Film Archive, Gala and Arco Film.

*Frontispiece: Rossellini talking about the voyages
of Christopher Columbus in* La Lotta dell'uomo
per la sua sopravvivenza.

Contents

Origins

Roberto Rossellini came from a family of builders. His father was an architect who worked on the plans for present day Rome. The eldest of four children, Roberto had an easy and uneventful childhood, marked by a passion for things mechanical. He built himself a workshop in which to construct his often ingenious inventions. The results have now moved into the sphere of legend: there is, for instance, the story told by Massimo Mida, one of Rossellini's assistants, that he tried, before World War II, to sell Bugatti the patent for an engine which would run on a mixture of water and benzine – a story that Rossellini says is untrue. One can, however, detect the legacy of this first enthusiasm in the things he has devised since 1959 to help in shooting his films. One is his version of the Pancinor, a modified 25/250 mm zoom with a remote control, which he works himself, and two interlocking motors which have a special braking effect and produce a deadbeat action free from oscillation; since *Era notte a Roma* (1960), he has used this in all his movies. Another is a special mixture of silver salts and glucose for partly silvering glass to form a mirror which makes it possible for him to combine action with scale models – a modification of the Schufftan process which allows the use of zooms. This was employed in *La Prise de pouvoir par Louis XIV* (1966) and *Socrate* (1970). Rossellini is at present concerned with devices involving high intensity lamps.

It was only after his father's death and a rapid decrease in the family fortune, that Rossellini became interested in the cinema. He was already familiar with the movies because in 1918 his father had built a cinema, the Corso, in the middle of Rome and later a second, the Barberini, both of which he visited very frequently. He later said that he had been struck by King Vidor's films, *The Crowd* (1928) and *Hallellujah!* (1929), 'perhaps the only "classical" films I had the opportunity of seeing at the time'. Rossellini had got to know many film people who had been his father's weekend guests. He decided to try his luck in the cinema and began by working for a brief period in editing and dubbing. Later he wrote a lot of screen plays anonymously. By way of apprenticeship, he used some money from his family to have a small studio set up at his villa at Ladispoli, near Rome. There he made some amateur shorts. The first of these seems to have been *Prélude à l'après-midi d'un faune* which, he has said, 'is not a visual ballet, as anyone who has not seen it might think. It is a documentary about nature.' It was banned as indecent by Fascist censors. After that he shot *Fantasia Sottomarina* in an aquarium he had built; the fish were controlled on strings, like puppets. A stream which he had noticed was the subject of *Il Ruscello di Ripasottile*. 'In these short films, one can trace my wanderings as a young man: the discovery of life as embodied in a buzzing hornet, or in the fish swimming in a stretch of water.' From the very beginning Rossellini seemed more inspired by his love of nature than attracted to the cinema for its own sake.

During this period, the Fascists were trying to attract young members of the middle class. Rossellini finally became involved in the official cinema by working on the screenplay of *Luciano Serra pilota* (1938), directed by Goffredo Alessandrini; it seems very likely that Rossellini re-shot most of the sequences directed by Alessandrini. It is not surprising that Rossellini was interested by the ideas of Francesco De Robertis, a naval officer and a writer preoccupied with the problems of screen drama. De Robertis was the spokesman for a direct cinema, using exclusively non-professional actors, more realistic and closer to documentary than to fiction films. *Uomini sul fondo* (1940), which De Robertis shot entirely aboard a submarine, made a deep impression on the young Italian directors of the time, including Rossellini. When De Robertis became chief of the film office of the naval ministry, he commissioned Rossellini to set up a documentary on the work of a hospital ship. In the course of shooting, this developed into a feature, *La Nave Bianca*. After the success of this film, he went on to become established in the professional cinema, directing *Un Pilota ritorna* and *L'Uomo della croce*.

Three Fascist Films

La Nave Bianca: *A sailor is wounded in a naval battle. He is given first aid and transferred to a hospital ship. There he is cared for by a nurse whom he later recognises as his pen-friend.*

Un Pilota ritorna: *A young Italian pilot is interned in a British prison camp after his 'plane has been shot down in action during the war against Greece. He is in love with a doctor's daughter and manages to escape during a bombardment. He reaches home, wounded, at the moment when news arrives of the Greek surrender.*

L'Uomo della croce: *On the Russian front during the summer of 1942, a saintly Italian chaplain aids a group of soldiers and peasants in a small village under Italian and Russian artillery fire. He is killed helping a dying man.*

The first shot of *La Nave Bianca* shows a warship's guns scanning; then we see other ships filing past on the horizon with the guns still in the foreground. This could be the beginning of a Russian film like *Battleship Potemkin*. But it is a propaganda film, produced by the Italian naval ministry under a Fascist government.

Even so, it is quite surprising that a film made under these auspices should begin with a scene in which some sailors are laughing over a letter sent to one of their companions by his pen-friend. 'She only talks about love and sacrifice – she must be a little teacher.' They look like typical Italians: one sports a huge

Still: Alessandrini's Luciano Serra pilota.

moustache and makes up rhymes, another blows his nose, another is angry because his pen-friend has not written to him, yet another is looking at a pin-up in a paper – a group of sailors who do not seem much disposed to make war. This first scene displays a fairly unusual realism: we have seen real sailors in Russian films, but they were used mainly as visual symbols able to express an idea with the help of editing. Here they are shown quite simply as sailors and regarded as human beings.

But the natural quality is sacrificed to rhetoric when the boy whose companions are making fun of him stands alone in the foreground, delightedly reading the letter from his 'little teacher', while the others gaze on enviously, and everything is bathed in slushy music. This sentimentality nullifies the simple and direct aspects of the next scene, when the sailor steals flowers from the officers' mess to give to his pen-friend. Afterwards he cannot get to meet her at the station where she is

Still: La Nave Bianca – *wounded sailors aboard the hospital ship.*

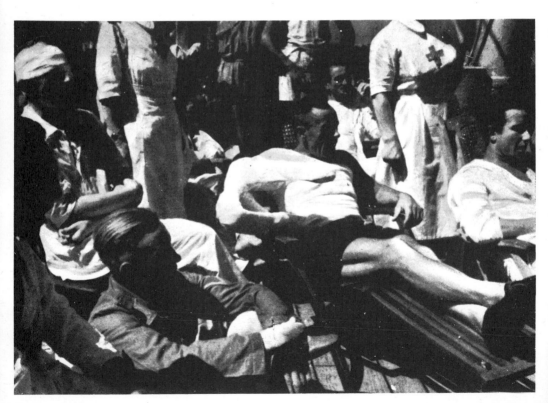

waiting for him; his guard duty is changed and he has to stay on board ship. The wailing violin music, too, is inconsistent with the feeling achieved when the boy changes out of his uniform into overalls and goes sadly off to his post. He is shown not as the star of a film, but simply as one individual in a group. We do not even know his name, Augusto Basso, until later, when he is wounded in battle.

Throughout, there is obviously a strong desire to combine the story with pure reportage. The ships' departure, with the farewells from the crowd, is filmed like a documentary. But the didactic spirit always returns. After some images of rather anonymous people, we see in the same shot a white-bearded old man, a beautiful young woman and a small child – Tradition, Beauty and Youth watch the departure of the ships which symbolise the Country. Then there is a general view of the crowd spreading out along the waterfront, a very authentic image, worthy of the best Soviet films. In the same way, the extreme documentary rigour of some scenes, like the one in which the wounded are taken off the hospital ship, the Arno, contrasts oddly with the finicky, *petit bourgeois* spirit which informs the treatment of life on board, especially the relationships between doctors, nurses and wounded men.

Affectation and austerity certainly make an odd combination in the last part of *La Nave Bianca*. It just happens that the nurse whose job it is to care for Augusto in the Arno is none other than his pen-friend (whom he still has not met). The end is played out in gestures, not words. The girl finds out who Augusto is when he begs her to write to his pen-friend; she will say nothing because now she is, in a sense, the girl-friend of all the wounded in her charge. And Augusto at last recognises the nurse as his pen-friend because she wears a medal, a present he sent before meeting her;

he will keep quiet when she appears evasive, only enjoying the simple pleasure of surprise. And their meeting ends like that, in uncertainty, with the image of a swinging door. But unfortunately, although this silent love-story is remarkable for its restraint, it also includes an exaggerated symbolism. The young girl comes to signify a completely aseptic purity, as Heroine, Mother and Country, reverberations made ridiculous by the playing of the untrained actors. In this way, all that is good in the film is immediately undermined by the most deplorable pretentiousness.

It would be unjust, as has been attempted, to attribute all the virtues of the film to Rossellini and all the faults to De Robertis, who is credited with story and supervision. The naval combat sequence has the same viewpoint and qualities as those built around the activities of sailors on board, or life in the hospital ship. The images which show the deployment of the machinery by which the shells are loaded are fascinating, but quite simply because the operation itself is fascinating and the director is content to film it as such without claiming to treat it from a particular viewpoint. Although machinery is the star of the second half of the film, the human side receives no less attention: the soldiers are frightened during the battle, and Augusto, who is shut in the hold, touches a horseshoe for luck as he hears the first explosions. A naval battle is horrifying, especially for men like Augusto who work the machines; as Rossellini has said, 'they only know they have to press a button when the red light shows and drop a lever at the green.' But here, even the fighting stops when Augusto is wounded and taken to medical quarters, though the struggle has to go on immediately after, because, in Mussolini's famous slogan, '*chi se ferma è perduto*'. During the operation on Augusto the ship goes back into battle with '*uomini e macchine un sol*

9

palpito' – a new slogan on which the camera fixes during the gunfire. At the end of the fighting the hospital ship is called to collect the wounded, while the captain congratulates the crew on their courage and speaks of '*nostri cari caduti*'.

Now, the didactic aim is obvious: a) to encourage a blind trust in superiors; b) to show that those wounded in battle are immediately cared for; c) to demonstrate that there must be no stopping until victory is attained. *La Nave Bianca* is not an ambiguous film: it sets out as a slightly sentimentalised documentary to show how anyone in the Italian navy who is wounded in battle receives every care and is at once sent home.

Un Pilota ritorna and *L'Uomo della croce* show an equally strong desire to escape from fiction in a search for the authenticity of reportage. Both show the fighting outside Italy and are built on the common theme of liberty, which later becomes one of the fundamental pre-occupations of Rossellini's work. In the first of these films (on which the supervisor, Tito Livio Mursino is none other than Vittorio Mussolini, brother of Il Duce), an Italian airman manages to escape from a prison camp in Greece; in the second, a small group of Italian soldiers, with Soviet prisoners and some Russian peasants, are in their turn imprisoned in an *izba* under Italian and Russian gunfire. With the impossibility of seeing *Un Pilota ritorna*, as the negative has been lost and no copies remain in Italy (though it seems that one still exists in Czechoslovakia), we must confine ourselves here to *L'Uomo della croce*.

A small child is wandering towards the door of an *izba* when bombs start exploding nearby. The child's terrified cries are heard even above the sound of the explosions. Unlike *La Nave Bianca*, the film does not present the effects of war as a scientific fact. Horror, wounds and death are the centre of interest, although the tactical movements and the tank attack are set out with the same documentary rigour, combined here with a remarkable sense of movement often reminiscent of Robert Aldrich's *Attack!* (1956). The important idea is a sort of brotherhood in suffering which unites the young Italians, shown in the first scene worrying about their future, with the Russian peasants, pursued by a war they do not understand, and with the chaplain who is to sacrifice himself for all of them.

The character of the chaplain assumes too symbolic a role because it never really escapes from the grips of propaganda: an end-title informs us that '*questo film è dedicato alla memoria dei cappellani militari caduti nella crociata contro i "senza Dio" in difesa della patria e per recare la luce della verità e della giustizia anche nella terra del barbaro nemico.*' But the behaviour of this priest is quite different from that of traditional Catholic heroes. The chaplain, an awkward figure, who hides timidly behind spectacles, is not very attractive: he helps the peasants, risks his life looking for water to baptise a baby, preaches brotherhood before God to the militant Soviet and dies at the end taking help to a dying soldier. But he still remains cold and distant. He sets out only to accomplish what he believes to be his duty. In spite of the end-title, the treatment of the enemy is fairly impartial: the political commissar, his companion and his men fight with genuine courage. Only the officers at the advance post are portrayed as the laboured stereotypes of the anti-Marxist cinema. Even so, one of these characters breaks free from the cliché by an act of extreme cowardice and becomes something really diabolical: the driver of the tank who reaches the *izba* with his disfigured face hidden in bandages and later shoots the commissar with a revolver. (There is a still more threatening echo of this almost

Dostoievskian character in the lame Tarcisio, who is the evil spirit of *Era notte a Roma*.)

But the ultimate meaning of the film is to be found in the actual construction. *L'Uomo della croce* begins with a very long panning shot which follows some birds flying free. This feeling for freedom conditions the whole film: the resting soldiers long for their distant homeland as much as the poor peasants who have been thrown off their own land by the war. The beings imprisoned in this world of destruction can have some fleeting moments of harmony; in a single sweep a long panning shot shows the starry sky, an owl and the chaplain holding in his arms a soldier with a shattered skull – a very searching movement that implies a provisional agreement between man and nature. It serves as leitmotiv later, when all of them, Italians and Russians, allies and enemies, are shut up in the *izba*. At the end, in an act of perfect charity, the priest lays himself open to gunfire in order to take help to the disfigured soldier, and thus finds this harmony again: falling, he loses his glasses (for the first time in the film) and looks suddenly younger – in a way becomes a child again. At this moment another long panning shot (like the one of the birds at the beginning) shows a herd of runaway horses bolting across the battlefield, and brings the film full circle in one curious, lyrical bound.

Roberto Rossellini's first three films, then, appear entirely subject to the demands of Fascist propaganda; they praise sailors, airmen, priests, the army, country and religion. In spite of all this, two at least display a remarkable feeling of directness. However, because of their 'ideology' they are not valued very highly and remain almost unknown. It must be granted that *La Nave Bianca*, *Un Pilota ritorna* and *L'Uomo della croce* make up the least consistent and most debatable part of Rossellini's work. But if they are considered apart from their set purpose, as *films*, they reveal a personality distinct from other Italian films of the time. Even if they misfire they do show sufficient respect for reality, care for objective *mise en scène* and perceptiveness over detail to raise them above the other Fascist films of the period.

Still: L.'Uomo della croce.

Desiderio

Paola, who comes from the country, is leading an easy life in town, when she is upset by the suicide of a friend. Giovanni helps her and then falls in love with her, but when he wants to marry her Paola feels that she is not worthy of him and goes back to her village, where her sister has just married. Both the husband, Nando, and Paola's former lover make advances to her. Attracted by Nando, but hurt by her sister's growing hatred, Paola, thinking that Giovanni has learned the whole truth about her past, throws herself off a bridge.

The first rendezvous between Paola and Giovanni takes place in a glass-house: a long tracking shot taken from outside, through the glazing, follows their movements within this unusual setting, expressing *visually* the idea that the young woman has entered a world which is not hers, but Giovanni's. Afterwards, while he is talking, Paola gradually falls asleep in her chair, enjoying a few moments of peace and respite, consoled by Giovanni's words. This cold, luminous existence, preserved artificially by the warmth of the sun, represents Paola's inner need, her nostalgia and her search for happiness, but at the same time it arouses a feeling of strangeness and threat.

Some moments in *Desiderio* have an astounding harmony of décor and action. Paola reaches her village by crossing the fields at the same time as a hearse, the silhouette of which remains on the horizon while she is embracing her sister. From this moment the return to nature takes on a disquieting, almost premonitory, significance. Towards the end, after a new incident with her former seducer, Paola is resting at home, wearing a luxurious dressing-gown which contrasts strikingly with the modesty, even poverty, of her country sur-

roundings. Small visual signs, then, suffice to show in an almost musical way how the trap is gradually closing in on the character.

The camera's sustained gaze at the girl's face reveals the internal course of her crisis, which is seen most clearly at three points in the film. After an orgy in her friends' apartment, Paola runs to her bedroom to look at herself in a mirror and immediately looks in *another*, as if she can no longer believe even in the truth of her own reflection. In the village, while grain is being fed to the hens, Paola confides in her sister and expresses to her the confusion she feels. This starts off a mutual confession, and the camera follows them in a single tracking shot as they talk at length – particularly convincing sequence – very much on the lines of Rossellini's later films, and surprising so early in his work. At the end, when her sister angrily orders her to leave, the camera fixes tenderly upon Paola's face, and her expression allows us to guess at the tragic act she is deciding upon. It is surprising just how similar Elli Parvo's face is to that of Lucia Bosè in *Cronaca di un amore*, which Antonioni was to shoot eight years later; in the same way, the orgy resembles the one in Fellini's *Il Bidone* (1955). *Desiderio*, then, seems to some extent to prefigure the way things were to move in the Italian cinema.

At its best, *Desiderio* is concerned with introspection through external signs, with watching behaviour as objectively as possible and not manipulating the realistic fundamentals of time and space – that is to say, with using the camera simply as a recording instrument; in a word, with observation. Unfortunately this is not the film's only concern. The village and its inhabitants are shown according to the rather facile conventions of the picturesque, in the traditional manner of *Quattro passi fra le nuvole* (Alessandro Blasetti, 1942), although the wedding procession does not compare badly with that in *L'Atalante*. And the plot may be tragic, but the laborious stringing together of characters and situations follows the most worn-out patterns of melodrama. The rather French romanticism when Nando and Paola go on a motor-cycle trip – the gloomy meeting adorned with clouds and reflections in water, symbols of an intimacy already lost – scarcely harmonises with the simple truth of some of the looks and gestures.

It is easy to explain these differences in style. Rossellini, who unequivocally disowns *Desiderio*, began shooting in July 1943, only to drop it some time later because of the war. Marcello Pagliero (who plays the engineer, Manfredi, in *Roma, città aperta*) began shooting again three years later. After a permit had been obtained from the Ufficio della Presidenza del Consiglio, *Desiderio* was seized by the police on the very evening of its première. The version subsequently shown seems to have suffered a number of cuts. The copies now preserved in Italy and France (a 16 mm copy in Rome and a 35 mm one in Toulouse) only differ in a short scene when Nando catches Paola naked when she is washing. This does not appear in the Italian version, but neither can be guaranteed faithful to the authors' intentions.

Nevertheless, *Desiderio* is still interesting in the light of Rossellini's later work. Paola's travels on her impossible attempt to return to her origins (which only brings her up against a terrifying lack of understanding) leads to the complete solitude found later in *L'Amore, Stromboli, terra di Dio* and *Europa '51*, and ends in an act as definitive, tragic and accusatory as the suicide of little Edmund in *Germania, anno zero*. Even in its mutilated state, *Desiderio* has to be given due attention because it both puts an end to Rossellini's discourse on war from the Fascist side and it gives a fairly unusual and nonconformist view of the moral chaos which overtook Italy in the last days of Fascist power.

Roma, città aperta

Hunted by the Gestapo, a Resistance leader, the communist Manfredi, seeks refuge in the home of Pina, a friend's fiancée. When she is killed by the Germans during a search, Manfredi is hidden by his mistress, Marina. She betrays him and he is arrested with Don Pietro, a priest who is also on the side of the Resistance. Manfredi dies without giving up any secrets under torture; the priest is shot.

During the German occupation of Rome, a little music-hall actress, who is a drug addict and has an ambiguous relationship with an elegant but unmistakable lesbian (and mistress of the Gestapo commandant), loves and afterwards betrays a communist engineer, chief of the Italian Resistance . . . In the Gestapo offices an Austrian deserter hangs himself and the communist is tortured to death, while in a sumptuous drawing-room nearby, a German officer, drunk but still lucid, lugubriously foretells the annihilation of Nazism . . . It would be possible to pick out an infinite number of episodes – tragic, funny (the statue of a saint which seems to be looking at the buttocks of a Venus in the shop where Don Pietro delivers a sum of money hidden in a book) or tragicomic (the make-believe last rites on the furious old man during the search). It is not even necessary to recall the later austerity of Rossellini's work in order to realise with blinding clarity that *Roma, città aperta* is the most melodramatic of neo-realist films.

Just as in *La Nave Bianca, L'Uomo della croce* and *Desiderio* (and probably *Un Pilota ritorna*, too), this melodramatic side serves a symbolic, even didactic intention. But this aim, which is part of the outcome of the previous films, in *Roma, città aperta* is only a point of reference that is constantly being questioned. A priest and a communist struggle together against the invaders: that is the source of edification. But it is not only edifying; it is historical fact about an actual moment of time in a clearly identified country: Italy under the German occupation. In the film this alliance is shown as something which has arisen by chance out of a definite historical situation. During a pause in the interrogation Major Bergmann tells Manfredi what the outcome of the alliance will be, the political future of the country. The scene is remarkable for sticking firmly to immediate reality without losing a clear consciousness that the present is fleeting and always ambiguous. The ideologies are provisional: communism and the Church struggle side by side but will be separated after the liberation; the S.S. are hangmen and torturers, but as officer Hartmann announces, they, too, will pass.

In *Roma, città aperta* only the present exists; the past has been wiped out and the future is represented only by the image of children going off into the distance in the final shot. The film records without judging: in his office, Bergmann shows the Rome chief of police a plan of the city, divided into four zones on the Schroeder system, which was applied by the Germans to other European cities and allowed them to carry out gigantic round-ups with the fewest possible soldiers. Here Rossellini's filmed chronicle records history, which now becomes important in his work. In his historical films from *Viva l'Italia!* to *Socrate*, the chronicle form is used as the basis for his re-examination of history.

The creative process behind *Roma, città aperta* works in two directions – from documentary to fiction to documentary again. It started out as a documentary – on 19 January

1944, Rossellini started shooting a short about Don Morosini, a priest and member of the Resistance, who was shot by the Germans. This was financed by an old lady who later agreed to put up the money for another short on the resistance activities of the children of Rome. From documentary it moved over to melodrama, in the same way as *La Nave Bianca*. But as in *L'Uomo della croce*, when the dramatic conventions are stretched to their limit and applied for the first time to a well-defined episode in contemporary history, we get back to documentary through Rossellini's concern to capture the

Frame stills: Roma città aperta. *Top row –*
Don Pietro, Hartmann reading L'Unità, Pina.
Bottom row – Manfredi, Manfredi with Pina,
Maria and the lesbian Ingrid.

fleeting reflection of appearances. In *Roma, città*
aperta, on the day before Pina is supposed to
marry Francesco, the building in which she is
hiding Manfredi is searched and Francesco is
taken off in a lorry. With a heart-breaking cry
she runs after it, only to be cut down by a burst
of machine-gun fire. Here, all the action is seen
from the outside, objectively. The camera con-

fines itself to watching a reality which is dramatic in itself, in the manner of reportage. This same quality of truth strikes us in the grey, bleak dawn when Don Pietro is shot and the children return to Rome.

This realism can be found at all levels in the film. We see up women's skirts and we see babies on their pots – two images which neo-realism has brought into the iconography of the cinema. But the documentary approach evidently goes much further than that. Everyone expresses himself in his own language, or in his own style: the conversations between Pina and Don Pietro on the Via Casilina and between Francesco and Pina on the staircase of the block of flats are two of the most moving scenes in the film, because they accurately capture a certain manner of speaking used by the people of Rome. Everyone in the film is totally identified with his character, even in the

Frames: Roma città aperta. *Left – Pina runs after the truck; Marcello with his mother's body. Above – Pina and Don Pietro in the Via Casilina.*

simplest gestures, but in its truthfulness his image contributes to that of the struggling community. As Maurizio Ponzi has pointed out, finally, there are no leading characters; all are heroes, and *Roma, città aperta* is summed up symbolically in a few particular faces: the disturbing face of Pina, the bloodstained face of Manfredi, the weeping face of Don Pietro. (Twenty-five years later, *Era notte a Roma*

identifies the tear-streaked face of Esperia, Giovanna Ralli, with that of Rome.)

Now it becomes easier to understand the significance of the décor. The film remains faithful to the geography of Rome as well as to its physical realities. The block of flats near the Via Casilina where Pina and Francesco live is actually very much as it appears in the film – workers' flats, put up by the Fascists for railway employees. It has a personality of its own, with its staircases, through which, during the search, the Fascists look up at the legs and bottoms of passing women, and with children playing

Frame: Roma città aperta – *the children return.*

on the terraces. It ends by becoming a character in its own right and an extension of the film's meaning; just as Pina, Manfredi and Don Pietro are tortured and killed, it is broken and destroyed. It becomes the symbol of its inhabitants and of the whole grieving city.

The great originality of *Roma, città aperta*, then, does not rest merely on the use of natural locations (essential in any case, because the studios were destroyed during the war) but on the way they are integrated into the film, and the way the non-professional actors identify with their characters; the way characters and setting become the film itself. It is very important to stress the absolute spontaneity with which this integration comes about. In other Italian films, like *Ossessione* (1941) or Mario Soldati's little known *Eugenia Grandet* (1946), success is achieved by a conscious effort of reconstruction. In *Roma, città aperta*, it is simply *discovered*, thanks to humble, careful observation. Everything seems miraculously to have been seen for the very first time, just as it did at the birth of the cinema.

Paisà

Sicily: A young girl points out the way to American soldiers who have just landed. She stays with one of them and is herself killed after seeing him shot by a German bullet.

Naples: A child goes to a puppet theatre with a drunken negro soldier and steals the man's boots. When the soldier catches up with him, the boy takes him home with him to the caves used by refugees at Margellina. The soldier runs away, frightened.

Rome: A drunken GI spends a night with a prostitute, not recognising her as the young girl he fell in love with during the liberation of Rome.

Florence: An English nurse goes to Florence to look for her fiancé, Guido, who has become a Resistance leader. She learns of his death from the lips of a dying partisan.

Romagna: Three American chaplains miraculously escape the war and reach a monastery; the monks fast for the conversion of the two chaplains who are Protestants.

Po: American soldiers are fighting with the partisans against the Germans. When the group is captured by the numerically superior enemy, the partisans are shot or drowned and an American who rebels against this is also killed.

From the start, the first episode gives a feeling of rediscovering the cinema. Separated from his unit during reconnaissance, the soldier, Robert, stays to keep watch in a deserted building with a young Sicilian girl, Carmela. He offers her a cigarette, which she refuses. He makes an unsuccessful attempt to start a conversation – 'the sea – *il mare*' – and there is a slightly comic misunderstanding when he takes her arm (to stop her going away, but Carmela thinks that he wants to make love to her and pushes him off). Then he sits down, takes off his helmet and tries to make himself under-

stood. Reflected moonlight shines off the sea through a window in the background. Robert talks about children and brings out a photograph of a girl which Carmela regards with a trace of jealousy, in spite of her apparent disinterest. The soldier notices her reaction and says, 'It's my sister.'

The beauty of this moment in the film is not achieved by any artistic manoeuvring. The camera keeps still throughout the long conversation, content to look and record, like a

Still: Paisà – *the Sicilian episode.*

film by Louis Lumière. A lot more is suggested than can actually be seen: the soldier's loneliness, his need to talk to someone, his longing for home and family, the girl's growing confidence – she distrusts him at first but gradually comes to feel secure for the first time in ages and flirts instinctively with him. We feel the growth of a tenuous understanding between these two and the sudden appearance of many hidden feelings, quite simply. To show all this with such economy of means is one of the great secrets of the cinema.

The whole of *Paisà* witnesses the same pressing need to portray a complex reality directly, at one go. A good example is the American soldiers' reaction when, at the end of the Sicilian episode, they find Robert's body and without knowing what has really happened, immediately assume that he has been betrayed by 'this Italian trash'. Other significant moments could equally be quoted: in the Naples episode, when the Negro GI begins to doze off, after singing the praises of his country, little Agostino points out, 'If you go to sleep, I'll steal your boots!', or in the Roman episode when, in a disturbing close-up, Maria explains her confusion to the American soldier who has come home with her to wash his hands: 'We have waited for you so long', the girl murmurs, and he answers, 'Yes, long time, *siamo qui.*'

The present-tense photographic observation, however, allows the audience to make distinctions or choices only at a higher level. When Maria has recognised the drunken soldier as the boy she greeted at the liberation, she gives him her address in an effort to bring back the past; the unhappy encounter ends with searing brutality in a couple of shots: the soldier talks to a friend and throws the paper with the girl's address on the ground while she waits hopelessly in the rain. The episodes set in Florence and the Po valley move in a series of leaps, leaving enormous gaps for the audience to fill

in themselves. In Florence, the nurse, Harriet, travels through a maze of deserted streets, of incomprehensible orders, of shots which might have come from anywhere, and of meaningless deaths. After the partisans and the American soldiers have been given supplies in the shape of a basket of eels by a family of fishermen, the party hears distant gunfire; back at the fishermen's hut, men and women lie dead and a half-naked baby is yelling incessantly. There is no explanation of how the Germans discovered the fishermen, any more than there is of how the baby remained alive. We see facts, each containing a world of ideas, which somehow summarise in a flash the spirit of the whole film, but straight away we go on to something else and that's that. Participation by the audience is greatly increased in this way, since we have to fill in the gaps and understand that other things exist beyond what we can see. By this expedient, sentimentality is ruled out. There is physically not time to mourn the lot of dead soldiers or abandoned girls: there is scarcely time for a shiver of horror before our attention is drawn to some other piece of reality.

Paisà is presented above all as simple reporting, but it can easily be seen now to express as personal a viewpoint as a film by Hitchcock. However, the audience is not obliged to identify with characters, but to examine events as closely as possible and with the deepest concentration. It is as documentary that one is first struck by the boats with which the partisans cross the Po marshes, and the apparently improvised pictures have such authenticity that they might simply be part of a newsreel. But gradually we are made conscious of the haunting landscape: the muddy swamp water, waves lapping against the wood and, stretching to the horizon, reeds which could hide a man. We finally notice that the horizon is at the same level in almost every shot. This simple fact is

Stills: Paisà. *Florence – Harriet and Massimo are stopped by the partisans. Po – American soldiers fight alongside the partisans.*

used to pick out one of the essential features of this countryside. André Bazin noticed that this consistent proportion of water to sky is the exact equivalent within the framework of the screen, of the subjective impression formed by these men who live on this flat surface between earth and sky and whose lives constantly depend on minute changes in their angle to the horizon.

In spite of the improvised, almost unfinished

appearance of *Paisà*, every shot in the film is very deliberate, made to fit an exact design. Harriet and her friend Massimo, who has come to Florence looking for his wife, study the city from a terrace where a civilian in carpet slippers, evidently interested in military strategy, is following with his binoculars some fighting which we are never actually shown. Then they go down the long staircase of the apartment block: their movement is followed relentlessly by the camera in a long pan which also takes in some tenants anxiously discussing the situation about which they know nothing. Throughout *Paisà* there is this will to show individual conflicts in the midst of collective ones, never to separate characters from their environment, and at all times to respect the immediate reality of events, giving them their full duration. This search by Rossellini to find an ideal continuity to form a medium for synthesis finds its logical outcome in the single-shot *plan-séquence*.

The setting of the Florence episode is as carefully planned as that of the Po episode. It is the means to show us the deeper significance of events. Harriet wants to be reunited with her fiancé, Massimo with his wife and daughter. In order to find them they have to get into the

German-occupied half of the city. The only route is through the Uffizi Gallery which leads out, long, deserted and menacing, to a huge square which is empty apart from a lorry and a few almost ghostly figures of German soldiers. With this extraordinarily unreal image, we pass to the other side of the mirror. From this moment, we are in a strange world with its own laws, which gets to look more and more fantastic: the cart with a Red Cross flag, carrying a wounded man or a corpse, the giant bottle that the partisans are dragging over the crossroads with ropes, the heap of ruins which take on disturbing shapes. Without having departed from the strictest realism, we have reached the depths of fantasy: a parallel world in the manner of Borges. The horror builds up without apparent system. The partisans are unable to understand each other. There are shots, but we do not know where they come from; the

struggle is against an enemy the more threatening because invisible. Two traitors are executed without mercy. A man who lies wounded in Harriet's arms suddenly reveals in his delirium that her fiancé is dead, and the news strikes her with the force of a stray bullet. The beauty of the empty town makes these terrible images even more obsessive. In spite of being pure reportage, the Florence episode of *Paisà* is one of the greatest horror movies ever made.

There is, then, in *Paisà*, a complete integration between people and surroundings, which authenticate and act as extensions of each other, working towards an expression of the deepest implications of reality. This creative process is not new; it is part of the heritage gained by modern art from the revolution in the novel, begun on one hand by Cervantes and on the other by Stendhal, Balzac and Flaubert. There is a famous passage in 'Le Père Goriot' (1834) which describes the character of Madame Vauquer:

'Her face, chilly as the first frost of autumn, her wrinkled eyes, with an expression that moves from the set smile of the dancer to the sour frown of the discounter of bills, *ultimately her whole person is an explanation of the boarding house, just as the boarding house implies a person like her.*' (My italics.)

With the visual nature of the cinema, this interrelation of character and décor was to become crucial. The accepted history of the cinema is so fragmentary and inexact that it is difficult to pinpoint the first directors consciously to follow this method, but it can be said to have reached its height with Murnau and Welles.

However, while this recreation of the world is achieved by a powerful effort of re-invention in Murnau and reconstruction in Welles, Rossellini succeeds spontaneously in *Paisà*, as if without intending to, by clinging faithfully and with humility to the simplest and most

Frames: Paisà – *Florence – the Uffizi Gallery; German soldiers; the wounded partisan with Harriet and Massimo.*

immediate reality, and by employing his faculty of synthesis, his instantaneous, intuitive grasp of the essential, which is absolutely unparalleled in the cinema. *Paisà* introduced a new standard of realism in films and, by virtue of this, is as revolutionary a work as *Citizen Kane*.

Each shot of each episode of *Paisà* in a way implies the whole film because all of them refer to its essential of a people struggling for liberty (which was latent in *L'Uomo della croce* and explicit in *Roma, città aperta*). The film is completely structured around this. Geographically, we travel up the country from Sicily to the Po. In time, we move from the landing in 1943 to the total liberation in 1945. Here the idea of placing the Romagna episode before the Po episode was a stroke of genius: the peace of the little monastery in Romagna, while men are fighting and dying in the marshes, further augments the dramatic power of the end with the bodies of the partisans falling in the water. (Another discovery: the three chaplains have been together for twenty-one months, the entire Italian campaign, in fact for the course of the film.) The order, then, makes us immediately aware that we are being shown a whole country at war, with the contrast of seeing, almost simultaneously, areas where there is fighting and areas which, by chance or by geographical position, have escaped the conflict; equally we become conscious of the passage of time, because peace does not reach everywhere at once. We are finally involved in quite a complex sensation: of seeing the whole of the country at once in plan, while also discovering that the image presented is not flat, but has depth and can be seen as a whole in section.

Paisà completes the process started in Rossellini's earlier films: it is now possible to see how his taste for the chronicle form led him to discover the cinema. *Paisà* is his first masterpiece, a masterpiece of neo-realism as well as one of the peaks of film history.

L'Amore

Una Voce Umana: *A woman telephones her lover, who has left her to marry a young girl of good family, and says her farewells in a long and upsetting monologue.*

Il Maracolo: *A crazy peasant girl meets a young vagabond whom she takes to be Saint Joseph. Beside herself with joy, she lets him seduce her. When she gets pregnant, she announces the miracle, believing in her simplicity that she is to bear the Son of God. The peasants laugh at her, and even the village idiots harass her. The mad girl flees and gives birth to her baby in a deserted little sanctuary.*

The object of *L'Amore* is clearly announced in the words which appear on the screen at the end of the credits: '*Questo film è un omaggio all'arte di Anna Magnani.*' The film begins with a close-up of Magnani (la Nanna, as she is affectionately called in Italy) looking at herself in a mirror (*Una Voce Umana*) and ends with

Stills: Paisà – Romagna. Below (frame) the American chaplain says grace. Left – the monks give thanks for the ending of the war.

another when she gives her breast to her new-born child (*Il Miracolo*). In a sense, the whole film is a direct consequence or an extension of the disturbing close-up in *Roma, città aperta*, when the weeping Pina on the eve of her death tells her fiancé of her confidence in the future. Anna Magnani is the first in the astonishing portrait-gallery of women in tears who are the symbolic key to Rossellini's films. The faces of Ingrid Bergman and Giovanna Ralli are the incarnations of the films they are in. There are other directors exceptionally identified with their actresses, but few can be like Rossellini, who slaves with as much patience as love to get the best out of them.

In *Una Voce Umana*, Magnani flounders in her bedclothes, howls at the telephone, winds the cord (her last connecting link with her lover) around her neck, and weeps for her lost love; in *Il Miracolo*, she is ridiculed by the idiots who scurry around her like spiders, drags herself along the ground racked with pain, and toils up to the mountain sanctuary. The striking thing about all this suffering, undergone in complete and savage solitude, is that it is so total. She goes so far beyond human endurance that she unknowingly reflects the suffering of all mankind and becomes, to some extent, the archetype of all earthly grief. This is a pre-eminently Christian idea and it is not by chance that certain images and gestures during the mad girl's journey in *Il Miracolo* remind us consciously or unconsciously of Christ's passion. She is insulted by the peasants, crowned with a wash basin and mockingly given a flower. Finally she undergoes the painful Calvary of her climb to the sanctuary overlooking the village.

Una Voce Umana is always dominated by the telephone around which the drama turns. The camera draws back to show the woman alone and lost in her room when she thinks that she has been cut off, and her movements and

sometimes broken and sometimes singing, her almost animal presence, her communion with nature (she lies on the ground murmuring '*che paradiso*', chews a stalk and after making love is happily awakened, bathed in a warm sensual light, when she is tickled by a goat), her joy, her tears. Shortly before her climb to shelter in the sanctuary, a panning shot links the little waterfall in the mountain and the mad girl who caresses her belly, moaning '*figlio santo*', as if to establish identification between them with the movement. In all primitive mythologies water is the source of life, an idea upon which, fourteen years later, Robert Rossen constructed the whole of *Lilith*. In *Il Miracolo* and in some of the later films, the countryside is given a value and prominence scarcely known in the cinema outside Murnau. It is never used as a pictorial element or as an extension of the characters' states of mind: the setting is a living, sensual environment, which surrounds people and relentlessly wears them down as water does rocks. Its existence is the result of the systematic faithfulness to reality which was the profound innovation of *Paisà*.

Although all the action of *Una Voce Umana* occurs in single place and the character is almost always in close-up, the details of the surroundings which enclose her are not without importance: right at the beginning a mirror presents the woman's face, to which a telephone is drawn almost magnetically; she picks it up, only to put it down immediately. A little later we notice that she is not alone, but has with her a dog, a present from her lover, which will be the only witness, albeit unheeding, of the drama. Its presence can only make the absence of the man she loves even more harrowing. The movement of the camera away during her first telephone call makes us feel very clearly that the set is a prison. Thus the whole piece takes on a style different from that of the original because of the viewpoint that these simple

gestures indicate clearly that her talking has been useless. Her words have had no effect, and she is already condemned to unremitting solitude. From here on, the interest is centred, not on the dialogue, but on her face and what she does; her grief and suffering are shown from a *moral* viewpoint. For this reason, the extreme lack of shame in the woman's confession takes on a completely different significance from that revealed by a simple reading of Cocteau's text for the original sketch. The aim of *Una Voce Umana* is not to bring off a feast of technical skill – we spend about forty minutes shut up in one room with one character. Instead it becomes the pretext for a documentary on a woman's suffering.

Although it is looked at from what we might call an ethical angle, this suffering is depicted with surprising sensuality. Everything in *Una Voce Umana* and *Il Miracolo* is carnal almost to the point of obscenity: Magnani's voice, changes in camera position impose.

The exterior, therefore, is examined in the hope of reaching the soul, with as much care for making appearances speak for themselves as for preserving the real duration. Being shot in very long takes, *Una Voce Umana* tends towards the ideal of the *plan-séquence*, even if it is not actually made that way. The same is true of *Il Miracolo*, especially in its most beautiful moments: the long monologue at the start (extending as it does that of *Una Voce Umana*): the scene in the church when the crazy girl gives way to a mysterious impulse to steal an apple; the scuffle in the square with the idiot who, infuriated, starts to kick the tin cans which hold soup for the poor. As in *Paisà*, the style arises out of a deliberate concern for the present, while remaining conscious of the

fleeting aspects of what is shown, in order to reach the essentials. The camera is expressive, then, not by adopting 'artistic' angles – which it never does – nor by imposing a definite point of view, except as with Hawks, to make us see things more clearly from eye level. (There is only one exception here, never to be repeated in the whole of Rossellini's work, the surprising high-angle shot as the girl climbs the church steps to give thanks for her pregnancy.)

L'Amore comes from widely differing sources: a Cocteau monologue and a story by Fellini, which is very similar to 'Adega' (1901) a novella by the Spanish writer Valle-Inclán which, in its time, became almost a *cause célèbre*. The two halves of the film, though, have basically the same source of inspiration. They are both tales of unrequited love, with the accent on a woman's loneliness, on a solitude reached at the end of an obsessive and painful

Stills: L'Amore – *Anna Magnani.*

27

journey. The fevered monologue delivered over the telephone to an invisible lover in *Una Voce Umana*, exactly corresponds to the poor peasant girl's long tirade of love at the opening of *Il Miracolo*, when she approaches the vagabond, calling him '*San Giuseppe bello, santo mio bello*'. The lover's voice is never heard on the telephone, and the tramp remains silent during the mad girl's speech: the love of these two women remains unanswered. One will be left to despair; the other, through her perfect humility (she murmurs all the time '*non sono digna*' when she thinks she is to become the mother of God and kisses the stones on the ground when she reaches the sanctuary), will experience the human joy of giving her breast to a child. However, it must be emphasised that for the Paris presentation of *L'Amore* in 1956, Rossellini removed the end of the film in which bells rang out in greeting as the peasants welcomed the birth of the new saviour. The film now ends with the mother's first words to her child '*mio santo figlio*'. Contrary, then, to the belief of Eric Rohmer, I prefer to think that by eliminating this final apotheosis the director intended to remain more humbly among the humans. *Una Voce Umana* takes place entirely indoors, the outer world being mentioned only to make its absence the more cruelly apparent: the woman goes to the apartment door in the misplaced hope that a car she has just heard is bringing her lover. Practically all of *Il Miracolo* takes place outside, beginning with an image in which Nature is smiling, but leading to another descent into hell. The two women remain prisoners and struggle to escape: again Rossellini's obsession with liberty.

L'Amore is striking both for its unwonted cruelty and its disarming tenderness. It is simultaneously an act of love by the director for his actress, a reflection on the human condition and an inspired experiment in the expressive possibilities of the cinema.

Germania, anno zero

Edmund, a boy of fifteen, lives in Berlin with his sick father, his sister Eva and his brother, Karlheinz, in wretched housing, for which they pay an exorbitant rent. Edmund does odd jobs to earn some money. He meets his old teacher, a former Nazi who gives him work in the black market, repeating that the weak must die and only the strong will survive. More and more convinced that his father's existence is useless, Edmund decides to poison him. He is not conscious of the gravity of his action until it is too late and commits suicide by throwing himself off the top of an unfinished building.

Germania, anno zero must, like the Florence episode of *Paisà*, be considered above all a horror movie. It is a film in the likeness of its hero, the young Edmund, a child who is prematurely aged: the other children do not want to play with him, and they are right because they understand that Edmund cannot really be one of them. At certain moments, for example, at home, when he decides to find other work, his face contracts into a menacing grin reminiscent of the change from Jekyll to Hyde. His closed, set features finally become horrifying and we feel a real sense of relief when, having completed his fatal action, he begins to play at dusk and becomes a child again.

Germania, anno zero begins with an endless tracking shot down an avenue of ruins: we are faced with a statement of calamity. We look objectively at a town destroyed – the beginning of the film is purely documentary. But as it goes on, the tracking movement becomes obsessive; it takes on a hallucinatory feeling. It is the start of a journey into a strange, un-

Photographs: Germania, anno zero – *the streets of Berlin. Above – preparing to shoot the sequence with the horse. Right (frame) – Edmund.*

known land, with its own laws, the like Florence of *Paisà*. A little later, a horse which has died in the street is shared out, and people carry off pieces of steaming meat. Human life is worth little more: the boy kills his father because the man has become nothing more than a mouth to feed, as well as to end his suffering. Like *Paisà*, the film reaches fantasy through realism. In the ruined Chancelry, boys earn food by selling records of Hitler's speeches to American soldiers. To convince a possible buyer, Edmund puts a disc on a portable record player. As the Führer's voice rings out through the ruins, the camera pans over damaged buildings; an old man and a child stop to listen, dumbfounded, to the voice which already belongs to a phantom from the past.

Right from the title shot of *Germania anno zero*, time is wiped out. The past is over; it is no more than a distant illusion, as easily forgettable as a dream. In the destruction of *Roma, città aperta* the children's return to the city indicates a future: here there is no longer a future, nothing but ruins and death: the first human beings we see are digging graves in a cemetery.

The characters, imprisoned in suspended time are also prisoners in space. Edmund, Eva, Karlheinz, their father, all the Germans are piled up in barely habitable housing, where five families have to share one flat at a ruinous rent. It is interesting to discover, in the depiction of the flat, all the social clichés of post-war Italian films: sick father, daughter on the verge of prostitution, son in hiding for fear of political reprisals, child left to his own devices. But although they represent familiar types, these characters are examined in a very remarkable way, observed in long, continuous takes by a camera that follows with great suppleness and never lets them go. The camera pursues Karlheinz and Edmund throughout the painful explanations at the beginning of the film, and its inescapable gaze serves to make us see more clearly how they are imprisoned by their surroundings. All of them deeply resent their lack of freedom, from which they are trying to escape. Eva spends the nights searching for a husband in the nightclubs; Karlheinz, afraid of ending up in prison because of his Nazi past, escapes into unreality within the four walls of the room where he has chosen to stay. Most unfortunate of all is the father, condemned by illness to remain immobile as he watches the disintegration of his family and his world.

Frames: Germania, anno zero – *Eva quarrels with Edmund; Edmund's despair.*

Edmund himself seeks escape the only way open to him, in the streets. But such freedom as he manages to find among the ruins is illusory, although it allows him a measure of escape from the suffocating atmosphere of the apartment. Life in the bomb-damaged streets of Berlin brings him back up against the same lack of freedom, the queues outside the food shops and the black market deals. He meets his former teacher, an ambiguous character who employs children as salesmen so that he can provide them for homosexuals. There is the youngster who sells soap in the underground and cheats the woman who buys it from him, and there are the young thieves who steal potatoes from a goods train. The environment denies Edmund any possibility of remaining a child by reminding him all the time of the need to lie, steal and defraud in order to feed himself and his family. Inescapable obligations are imposed on him, which to others seem inappropriate for a child of his age: at the beginning of the film he is thrown out of the cemetery where he is digging graves, because the employer thinks he is too young for the job (although he isn't too young when it comes to helping his family). He seeks an escape into a world of fantasy, the railway tunnel where the young thugs hide, but has no success in joining their unreal community, where he is always treated as a stranger. Everything goes to help make him easy prey to the false ethics of Nazism, according to which only the strong will manage to survive: but it will be precisely his one act of force – poisoning his sick father – that brings about his destruction. In this respect, *Germania, anno zero* can be seen as a documentary on the way an environment can slowly mark a face, distort its features and finally destroy them.

The most striking thing about the poisoning scene is that it is not a cadenza in the dramatic conflict: it has the growing funereal splendour that has since been seen in Douglas Sirk's *Written on the Wind* (1956) and *A Time to Love and a Time to Die* (1958), following, as it does, the old man's heartrending confession to his son. In a few moments we see the full depth of misery in which Nazism has left men, their families and the country as a whole. However, the scene is not notable simply for its dramatic quality, but for the fact that the child's act is shown as just another of the things he has done since the beginning of the film. In the poverty of the apartment, the father misses the food he was given in hospital, and slipping the deadly medicine into his tea is no different in Edmund's mind from stealing coal, or obtaining merchandise to pay his family's rent – actions justified

by the instinct for survival and the desire to help his own family. But, being motivated by class ideology and the false ethics of Nazism, this new action becomes monstrous. The circumstances shown in the film are presented not from a purely dramatic viewpoint but from a moral one.

The poisoning can be seen as the moment when *Germania, anno zero* really begins. Everything leading up to it is organised in a rather traditional way, though with great coherence. Its purpose is to provide, with the greatest possible clarity, a moral viewpoint on a straightforward dramatic conflict: the repercussions of a monstrous act within the mind of a child. The enormous difference between *Germania, anno zero* and the films we are used to seeing about abandoned children is thus self-evident.

The rest of the film is an extended view of Edmund's aimless movements until his meeting with a death that has been waiting for him a long time. After his father's death, we see him abstractedly playing little games in the dusk (an astonishingly accurate observation: as soon as he is finally cut off from his roots, he is in a sense freed and reverts to childhood). He tries to join the group of young thieves who shelter in the tunnel. On the stairway of the flats, it seems for a moment as if he might give in to the temptation to go home. The next day, he visits his old teacher to free himself by revealing the crime he has just committed. Now the action is moving forward in leaps, leaving enormous gaps – where did Edmund spend the night, what did he do? – that definitively remove any sense of chronology, which has been vague, if not actually absent throughout the film. This abrupt, halting course has little in common with the literary fluency of much of the cinema; it arises directly from the same concern with synthesis as in *Paisà*, from the same desire to lay bare reality in order to reach the essential.

Here, this essential is to show how Edmund is forced by his act into a solitude from which he has no escape (just as the mad girl's pregnancy separates her from the peasants in *Il Miracolo*, which was shot after *Germania, anno zero*). He is rejected by his horrified teacher, as he is by the kids playing – he is no longer a child, for he has killed his father. He goes into the deserted ruins of a church, but religion can no longer give him any help.

The profound disturbance that can be seen in Edmund is not treated according to the conventions of psychological analysis, but from what is visible externally and always from actions that seem to be of little or no significance. The boy hops along and climbs a half-finished building – the only portent of the

Frame: Germania anno zero – *the teacher's horror at hearing of Edmund's crime.*

future we are given in the film. He plays with the head of a hammer as if it were a gun; several times he jumps into a patch of light shining on the ground, then stops playing a moment to look up at his home; he takes off his jacket to help him slip down a beam he is using as a slide; at the end, he covers his face with his hands as if dazzled by a sudden revelation and with a cry, throws himself into space. The unexpectedness of this decision shocks us; it defies the conventions of naturalistic cinema, which try to explain everything by the dramatic stringing together of a number of calculated events. But on the basis of its own structure, *Germania, anno zero* wants not to explain but to show.

Right from the beginning, we have a strong feeling of the genuine love and respect with which Edmund is depicted: he is never viewed with pity or condescension. This love and respect allow an objective examination from the outside of the child as he really is; we have no right to impose ourselves upon him, to interfere with his reality. We must therefore get to know him entirely by his actions and movements in their real environment. This moral discipline implies another concept of realism, one which attempts to reveal an internal experience through external behaviour – here through the games of a prematurely aged boy, which take him back to childhood, are the expression of painful search, the meaning of which can be understood only after the fatal, blinding moment of truth. Rossellini's method has an authenticity which the logical explanations of traditional drama lack.

But where does the truth begin and end? The cinema's victory over appearances, its success in revealing the internal through the external, finally comes up against failure because the conquest is partial and fleeting; it must always remain open to question. *Germania, anno zero*, like all Rossellini's later films, is a meditation on the essence of cinema and the relations between the film-maker and the world. This will become more and more conscious, an endless search to uncover a reality which must be pursued, however gropingly, to reach those miraculous revelations which can break through the impenetrability of people and things. *Germania, anno zero* remains a peculiarly moving film, not only for its disturbing account of post-war Europe, but also because it signifies that its author has made a definitive choice: after the decisive experience of total cinema in *Una Voce Umana*, he has renounced finished, perfect works for ever, in order to seek out another course, another cinema, which as Jacques Rivette was able to write a few years later 'opens a gap through which the whole cinema must pass or die.'

Frame: Germania anno zero – *before the suicide.*

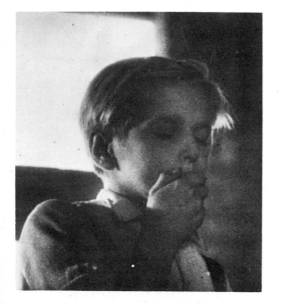

La Macchina Ammazzacattivi

In a small village in post-war Italy, the photographer Celestino receives from an unknown old man, whom he takes for a saint, the ability to kill evil-doers by simply photographing their image with his camera, which leaves them petrified on the spot. Celestino uses his formidable gadget to liquidate the corrupt village authorities, one by one. He becomes more and more set on the extermination of everyone who is wicked, but he comes to understand the impossibility of distinguishing good from evil. He tries to punish himself, first destroying the man who gave him such terrible power. Celestino discovers that the alleged saint is just a minor demon prowling the earth to earn good points with his master. When the photographer forces him to make the sign of the cross, an explosion puts everything back the way it was.

The film begins with a hand filling an empty space with the elements of a puppet theatre and transforming it into a set of a village, while the voice of the puppet master presents the characters and sets the scene. From the start, Rossellini imposes distanciation suitable for a fable; at the same time the action is placed in a specifically Italian context, that of the Commedia dell'Arte. At the end, the same hand removes the characters and their setting while the narrator recites the moral of the tale, extracting the meaning of the story in the same spirit of popular humour and wisdom: 'Cultivate the good without going too far, reject evil if you want to be saved, do not rush to judge and think twice before punishing.'

In the first scene of the film, an old man walking along the street is bowled over by a

car, but instead of being hurt, he quite simply disappears. A little later, this mysterious character turns up again, in a Southern village, among the faithful at a religious procession to celebrate the miracles of the patron, Saint Andrea. *La Macchina Ammazzacattivi* opens, then, with every appearance of fantasy, though this is always associated with reality: the procession looks as if it is taken from a newsreel; the supernatural power of the old man, which is capable of petrifying the policeman, Agostino, on the spot, works through a commonplace instrument devoid of mystery – a still camera.

Unlike another cinematic fable, *Miracolo a Milano* (1951), *La Macchina Ammazzacattivi* is specifically placed in time and space. At the beginning, an American ex-soldier returns to a village in the south of Italy, with the intention of building a hotel on land he had spotted during the fighting; the action takes place in the political, economic and social confusion of a country during the trying post-war period. In the Vittorio De Sica film, the Milan Duomo appears only as an element in the décor; here, village life – the catching and marketing of fish, the religious celebrations and popular festivals – is treated with documentary objectivity, and becomes the centre of the story, an integral part of the film's sunny, sensual vision.

In this well-defined historical context, the comedy elements can achieve the greatest significance. In a pause at the village council meeting, the mayor announces to his American associates that they will get the concession to turn the local castle into a hotel. The news is greeted ironically with Mussolini's slogan '*Vinceremo*' (which was also used by the Allies). The Americans arrive at their new place with the mayor, and a fine statuette – '*tedesca o americana*' – is found in the lavatory. All this is treated with consistent, sometimes rather black, irony: on their arrival in the village, the Americans admire a rock-strewn landscape as a good setting for the hotel; this was the scene of bloody fighting during the war, and they comment that 'the bodies can be taken somewhere else.' The American colonisation of Europe after the war later inspired other, similar films from the Latin countries, including Luis G. Berlanga's *Bienvenido, Mr Marshall* (1952) from Spain. Berlanga's earlier films, particularly, are in the same lazy and typically Mediterranean vein as *La Macchina Ammazzacattivi*.

Although regarded with the same affection as all the other characters, the country people are hardly treated with more benevolence. We see the old women looking with disapproval on the beautiful American visitor sun-bathing half-naked on the beach before admiring male

Frames: La Macchina Ammazzacattivi. *Left – the old man appears. Right – Romeo and Giulietta; Celestino at work.*

eyes (a little scene which might be the inspiration of the tragic conflict in *Stromboli, terra di Dio*), the lovers – Romeo and Giulietta – and their ridiculous elopement, the equally ridiculous council meeting at the town hall, the widow of a local poet, demanding a statue in memory of her husband. The huge sums of money which come to the village through the intervention of the unknown old man, the miraculous catch of fish, the eagerly awaited State subsidy, and the legacy left by the rich Amalia, bring out everyone's most mercenary appetites. The mayor thinks of nothing but his deal with the Americans; the other members of the council have their own interests; even the priest thinks of his new church instead of his poorer parishioners. But the poor themselves do not escape the corruption. When it is learned from Amalia's will that she has left all her wealth to the three poorest old men in the village, those closer to qualifying present themselves with false credentials. In this way all of them are reduced to grotesque puppets, the most unusual being undoubtedly the mysterious visitor whom Celestino exposes as a genuine devil complete with horns and a tail.

The absurd, then, is more prominent in *La Macchina Ammazzacattivi* than it is in any other Rossellini film. Not only does the film contain the most uproarious comedy, but for the first time there are real gags. Although the policeman, Agostino, gets petrified right in the middle of the procession, Celestino is still suspicious of the remarkable power given him by the old man. He decides to put it to the test, but believes in the saints and the devil like a good Southerner and only dares to try out the gadget on an animal, a donkey, which is naturally turned into a statue after some pitiful braying. Angry with the mayor's secretary who is trying to withhold Amalia's will, so that the civic authorities can profit instead of the village, Celestino photographs him, leaving him motionless while he goes off across the square with the old lady's funeral procession. Even the mayor ultimately suffers the same fate during the reading of the will, which Celestino has recovered. The photographer copies the only image of the mayor that he has, as a naked baby. The Americans move house for the third time in their stay. They are received as guests of honour, and in a real burlesque ballet they are shown the marvels of the villa – the great hall, the ancestral portraits and finally the petrified body of the owner, another victim of Celestino's justice.

Frames: La Macchina Ammazzacattivi – *the donkey on which Celestino tries out the potential of his gadget; Celestino with the priest, and fighting with the doctor.*

But making fun of death is not always amusing. The moral of the tale, in spite of the wise, quiet joy of the ending, is still very bitter. Thrown out by Agostino, the policeman, during his work at the procession, unrecognised by the mayor at the civic council meeting and beaten up by an unknown thief (actually one of the relatives), who has made off with Amalia's will, Celestino discovers to his cost that it is 'dangerous to steal from the rich', as he is told by the village doctor. It is also risky to join in a battle of wits with them: when Celestino attempts to convince the mayor that the inheritance should be democratically shared among all the villagers, his is given a lecture on economics: 'capital shared goes down to nothing and is lost . . .' His belief that the social order is unjust, starts Celestino administering justice, as it were, overruling God. His successive failures stem from the absurdity of his undertaking. He cannot keep his gadget under control as he should: while making an enlargement of a family photograph,

he fumes at Amalia without really wanting to, but when she emerges from her indifference for a moment and insults him, he puts her out of action definitively. His justice does no good at all. For one thing the wicked go on being wicked, and for another, in petrifying Amalia he even brings about evil in arousing the greed of the old lady's relatives. He is also unable to distinguish good from evil: not until the end, and then only by chance, does he discover that the alleged Sant' Andrea is actually a demon. With his boundless justice, Celestino even goes so far as to transform good into evil: his apparatus changes from an instrument of justice to a harbinger of death when, scandalised by the general show of covetousness, he decides to kill everyone. He beats the doctor unconscious for wanting to put an end to his madness. Celestino is human and has not the right to judge.

We can also reach the moral from a rather unusual angle, concerning almost the essence of cinema. It is difficult to believe that this 'evil-destroying machine' was chosen unselfconsciously as the subject. The deadly power of this still camera is exercised by photographing not real people, but merely their image in a photograph. The difference is very important if you consider that a photograph, in recording appearances fixes them at a moment that no longer exists, lost in the memory of a life already past. A photograph, then, encloses an instant of '*la mort au travail*', as Cocteau called it. Godard has always been obsessed by this subject, which has cropped up from time to time in his films, since *Le Petit Soldat* (1960). It is not difficult to understand how, in conjuring up this instant of mortality, which is fleeting and yet fixed in time, the devil can have the power to bring about the death of the subject. But the tale has a further significance: it shows the dubious nature of reality in the cinema, which can reproduce life perfectly, but purely from an external point of view; it preserves only the appearance of life. Probably, *La Macchina Ammazzacattivi* touches on this problem without any express intention, but it is interesting, all the same, that Rossellini should have remembered it fifteen years later in developing the central theme of the sketch *Illibatezza*, his last work intended for the cinema. The photographer Celestino brings about as many misdeeds as Uncle Julius/Jerry Lewis in *The Family Jewels* (1965): such disastrous results are unavoidable when you take it into your head to manipulate reality and 'artistically' alter it. Thus, the moral becomes very simple: life must take preference over the cinema.

After the austerity of *L'Amore* and *Germania, anno zero*, *La Macchina Ammazzacattivi* has unrestrained fantasy, energetic action, and an abundance of characters who enter, leave and are rearranged endlessly. It is a film about confusion of all kinds; human, social, political, economic, artistic. It must have interested Rossellini as a chance to give free rein to his inspiration, to reflect a moment both in the history of his country and also his own personal history. But this same transitory aspect drove him in a different direction, to the adventure of *Stromboli, terra di Dio*, and he left *La Macchina Ammazzacattivi* without finishing it. Shooting was completed by his assistants, Massimo Mida and Renzo Cesana, but the film was not seen until four years later, when another company, Fincine, took it over and edited it. *La Macchina Ammazzacattivi* occupies a similar position to *Desiderio* on the list of unfinished films, written off by their director, but still of interest for what they disclose about his personality and his idea of the cinema.

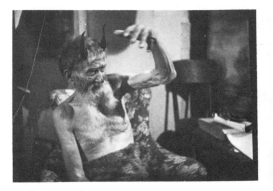

Frames: La Macchina Ammazzacattivi – *a final surprise; the mysterious old man turns out to be a minor league demon.*

Stromboli, terra di Dio

To get out of an internment camp after the war, Karin, a Lithuanian refugee agrees to marry Antonio, a young fisherman from the island of Stromboli, and himself an ex-prisoner of war. She goes to Stromboli with her husband but cannot adapt to the harshness of life there, the barrenness of the area or the hostility of the inhabitants who look upon her only as an intruder. Pregnant with Antonio's child and rebuffed when she finally makes an effort to become accepted, Karin is even more a prisoner than she was before. After a violent eruption of the volcano, she tries to seduce the young lighthouse-keeper as a means to escape. She climbs over the slopes of the volcano to reach the port on the other side of the island, but gets lost and falls asleep. She wakes up sobbing and calls on God to help her.

Nature in its full splendour rules *Stromboli, terra di Dio*. With the harshness of the land and the fury of the volcano, man's only friend is the sea, a kindly element and the provider of food; Nature is at its most benevolent and sunny in the tunny fishing sequence. During the eruption, the sea gives refuge for the boats which shelter the island's terrified inhabitants (but cutting them off from the mainland and the world, it is the main cause of Karin's isolation). *Stromboli, terra di Dio*, with its combination of the three basic elements of earth, fire and water, is the Rossellini film most concerned with the universe; Man's dependence upon Nature is portrayed with a skill worthy of Robert Flaherty and *Man of Aran* (1934).

All this places *Stromboli, terra di Dio* among the greatest of documentaries. But the film does not operate only as documentary: it begins with Karin in the camp and ends with her beside the volcano – it *is* Karin. All the same, it would be wrong to conclude that its concern is with the scrutiny of an individual, as the self-styled neo-realist critics believed at the time. *Stromboli, terra di Dio* – and the tunny fishing sequence is the most striking example – sets out to be a study of the relationship between a woman and the world. If either element is considered in isolation, the film becomes meaningless.

It begins with a pan past women in an internment camp, ending on Karin. The last shot is a pan in the other direction, showing gulls flying free over the volcano. Yet again in Rossellini, liberty is the central concept of the film. Karin is a victim of the war: during the interview with the chief immigration officer, a single disturbing close-up is enough to show the spiritual marks that the war has left on her. Her mental imprisonment is echoed by the physical confinement of the camp, from which she feels she has to escape at any price. Failing to obtain a visa for Argentina, she marries

Frame: Stromboli, terra di Dio - *Karin (Ingrid Bergman).*

Antonio, whom she does not love, and goes with him to Stromboli. On their arrival, Antonio shows her his wretched house and opens the window; all she can do is go out and look at the sea, which now separates her from the world. She has merely escaped from one prison into another. In the end, she will be literally imprisoned, when her husband nails planks over the doors and windows to prevent her leaving him.

After her first night on Stromboli, Karin is drawn out from her hovel by the sound of a child crying; as she goes to look for it, she sees the island for the first time since her arrival. Shown like this, alone and lost in the landscape, Karin is caught in a real labyrinth. This feeling extends to her relationship with the people of Stromboli. With the exception of their kiss through the barbed wire of the camp, we never see any physical contact between Karin and Antonio. They sleep in separate beds, but after a time Karin gets pregnant, and thus becomes even more of a prisoner than before. The young fisherman thinks only of his work, remaining unaware of Karin's attempts to improve their home. However, he behaves according to the conventions dictated by local custom and has no hesitation in beating his wife on two oc-

casions – after she has put her arms around a man on the beach to stop herself falling in the water and after the boys' serenade. Karin's relationship with the other inhabitants is made more difficult because life on the island is so primitive. For the men, she becomes an object of desire; the women treat her with distrust which turns into open jealousy in the face of the interest their men are taking in this foreigner. One of them even gets angry with Karin for talking to her sick husband . . . The children, who are not bound by convention, are unable to communicate with Karin, because she can only speak English. Religion, which is so important to the people of Stromboli – the Mass, the 'grazie a Gesù e a Maria' after fishing, the prayers to calm the volcano – cannot give her any appreciable help, nor can the priest. Not even the kindliness of the old man who has come back from America is of any use to her, because by this time Karin has realised that her true enemy is the island, the symbol of her imprisonment. Henceforth the only possible dialogue is between her and Stromboli.

The geography of the island imposes upon its inhabitants a very hard way of life and a very rigid set of rules to live by, which Karin is not willing to hear or allow. 'La terra è dura', the priest tells her when she arrives, but she does not understand: 'Come si dice terra in inglese?' Antonio tries to explain, without success – lack of communication is first apparent on the level of language. The land is poor; fishing and hunting are the only ways for the village to obtain food. But Karin cannot hide her disgust when her husband gives her a dead fish and hits him furiously when he kills a rabbit. When the men are fishing for tunny, Nature is made to seem magnificent though terrifying, but Karin, fascinated by the fish blood and horrified by this explosion of life and death after the fishermens' quiet wait in the sun, is not conscious of the beauty. Stromboli

Frames: Stromboli, terra di Dio. *Opposite – in the camp. This page – the people of Stromboli; Karin and the priest.*

is for her a mysterious universe, subject to strange laws that are beyond her understanding. When she is sobbing in her home, other cries answer like magical echoes; when she lights the kitchen fire, the volcano starts to erupt as if it had always been waiting for that signal – the smallest human action seems to have strange and enormous consequences.

Karin's only moments of happiness on the

island come when she gives herself up spontaneously to the protection of Nature, however terrible it may be – for example, when she chews on a piece of grass as she looks for the lost child, or when she goes to sleep on the beach in the sun, or makes her first and only attempt at joining in the life of the village by putting her house to rights. She puts up new curtains, arranges plants around the place and paints flowers over the white walls. This scene, one of the most beautiful in the film, with the woman's simple movements followed lovingly by the camera, also indicates her mistrust of the world surrounding her. She is really trying to create her own setting, a refuge in which to hide, for want of any other logical retreat.

Karin does not discover the world from which she is trying to escape until after her great crisis, which follows the volcanic eruption. She runs out of the house to try to leave the island for ever, but in her climb over the mountain to reach the harbour at the other side she becomes lost. Blinded by the gases from the volcano, Karin lives through a night of fear, crying herself to sleep, alone, like a child. This is the turning point in the film's strange dialogue between a woman and an island, and is expressed with outstanding sensuality. The tears and sobs of an actress are never likely to be as carnal, as Ingrid Bergman's in *Stromboli, terra di Dio*. Karin wakes up in the early morning and finds that she is feeling tranquil and relaxed. Strikingly beautiful (in no other film is Bergman as lovely as she is at this moment), she looks around her and is forced to exclaim 'What beauty!' She goes back up the slope of the volcano and looks down to the village at her feet as if she were seeing it for the first time. She murmurs 'I can't go back!' and bursts into sobs, calling on

Frames: Stromboli, terra di Dio – *Karin on the island.*

Frames: Stromboli, terra di Dio – *Karin tries to escape. Bottom – the prayer.*

God for help.

Although the narrative framework of *Stromboli, terra di Dio* is disconcertingly simple, the film itself is fairly obscure and difficult to interpret. The theological conclusion is only relative, and the structure of the film itself makes it more pantheistic than Catholic. This is in spite of the quotation at the beginning (*Hanno chiesto di me quelli che pure non mi cercavano, mi hanno trovato coloro che non domandavano di me* – I am sought of them that asked not for me; I am found of them that sought me not. Isaiah 65, i) and despite Karin's final entreaty – 'God, my God, help me! Give me the strength, the understanding and the courage!' We are not allowed to draw any conclusions as to whether the woman will come back in submission to the village, escape from the island, or finish up dying lost on the mountain. We only know that from the moment she recognises that she is enslaved by her environment, she becomes in some way free. Given the fundamental dramatic idea, nothing would be easier than to end the film with a fine, sparkling coda. *Stromboli, terra di Dio*, however, is limited to a faithful account of a crisis; it simply watches the crisis blow up and witnesses its occurrence. The ending calls for interpretation by the audience: the flying gulls in the last shot seem equally to celebrate freedom and the beauty of Nature and this *terra di Dio* – the idea of which is very important to the author, if you remember that it appears as a separate title in the credits, after the word *Stromboli*.

But a fundamental contradiction in the cinema justifies our asking whether the beauty of this world is the work of God, or quite simply the result of the director's art. Without departing from the most rigorous documentary approach, he achieves a purity of line and a spontaneous skill in composition reminiscent of the later work of Matisse. What is clear is that Rossellini is no longer primarily concerned to tell a story, but to investigate feelings and analyse personalities. At the time, Rossellini made a statement of principles which add up to a manifesto:

'I need a depth which perhaps only the cinema can provide, both the ability to see characters and objects from any angle and the opportunity to adapt and omit, to make use of dissolves and internal monologue (not, I might add, Joyce's stream of consciousness, but rather that of Dos Passos), to take or leave, putting in what is inherent in the action and what is perhaps its distant origin. I will combine my talent with the camera to haunt and pursue the character: the pain of our times will emerge just through the inability to escape the unblinking eye of the lens.'

Francesco, giullare di Dio

Francesco (i.e. St Francis of Assisi) comes back to Santa Maria degli Angeli from Rome, journeying with his friars through the rain. When they are driven out of a hut, he begs the brothers' forgiveness for abusing their obedience. While the monks are finishing the chapel, Brother Ginepro returns naked, after making a present of his habit to a poor traveller. The elderly Giovanni, called The Simple, is prompted to join the community by his wish to be like Francesco. In the course of a visit from Sister Chiara, Brother Ginepro arrives naked again and confesses that the previous night he was tempted by the Devil. Later, Brother Ginepro cuts the foot off a pig to feed a sick brother. That evening, Francesco meets a leper and kisses him. Brother Ginepro receives Francesco's permission to preach and arrives at the camp of Nicolaio, the tyrant of Viterbo, whose cruelty he overcomes with his perfect humility. Francesco teaches Brother Leone that bearing injuries and blows is an example of perfect joy. Francesco sends his brothers out to preach far and wide.

This is a film about harmony. There is perfect accord between Man and Nature, heaven and earth. The earth, the fire and the water are no longer man's enemies, as they were in *Stromboli, terra di Dio*, but are his allies and accomplices. Fire, for instance, becomes Brother Fire, when Francesco asks Brother Giovanni, who is set on beating out the flames that are about to consume his master's tunic, 'Why do you want to do it harm?' Fire is also the visible sign of Brother Ginepro's perfect charity. He literally sets fire to the camp of the tyrant, Nicolaio, a magic and mystical conclusion to their odd

Still: Francesco, giullare di Dio.

encounter. Even soaked with rain when they reach Santa Maria, even when the country people cannot hear Brother Ginepro's words over the roar of the waterfall, the monks love and respect water, as belonging to Nature and God. They have deep-seated ties with the earth and even seem to have grown out of it. Men and animals are established in this privileged world in simple harmony. Francesco talks with the birds while Ginepro fondly addresses the pig whose foot he wants to cut off: 'What a chance for us to do good . . .'

The interesting thing about the little Franciscans in the film, particularly in comparison with the sort of priest we are used to seeing in movies, is their energy. They are almost never still or inactive, but always doing something, like building their hut or making small objects, because, as one of them explains, 'doing things by oneself is a way of getting to know about life.' Sweeping out the porch of their chapel, planting corn – the rustic nature of each action and each gesture indicates an angelic simplicity. They return home singing,

and cut each other's hair, jostling for a better position in the chapel. At all times they display a perfect joy that expresses itself in their games. Giovanni the Simple plays on the chapel bells, Brother Ginepro plays at swinging with the children after his unsuccessful sermon, the brothers balance on each other like jugglers to pick fruit. This idea of juggling reflected in almost all their actions, reveals a faith as strong and simple as that of David, the king who, as the Bible tells us, danced before the Arc of the Covenant to please the Lord. The idea of these 'jugglers of God' was so important that the

director incorporated it in the title to make his intentions clear, and they unconsciously embody a profound concept of religion and the Universe.

These naïve, untutored men, who do not exactly have the gift of words, can express faith only through gestures and actions. Because 'divers are the ways of the Lord', the monks inquiry about which way to go is answered by Francesco having them spin round on a crossroads until they all fall down. Each is set off down the road which points in the direction in which he has fallen. This is the astonishing last sequence of the film in which a long pan draws together men, earth, water and sky in harmony. Sanctity is also revealed by actions. Francesco picks up a small bird that has fallen; he teaches prayers to Giovanni the Simple; he kisses the leper. Ginepro gives his habit to a passer-by and then lets another rob him; he wants to give his own foot to the pig in return for the one he has cut off to feed a sick brother; he bears the blows he receives in Nicolaio's camp because 'Souls are won over

by example, not with words.' All these actions portray an absolute purity, a perfect charity, a total giving of oneself to others. It is significant in this respect, that Brother Ginepro, through his qualities, gradually becomes the central character of the film and holds it together dramatically. He receives Francesco's permission to preach, only on condition that he unceasingly repeat '*Bò, bò, bò, molto dico e poco fò*', and leads the film to its conclusion, the excellent episode of his encounter with the tyrant which is really a film within the film.

Although their instincts direct them away

Stills: Francesco, giullare di Dio.

from reality, the characters of *Francesco, giullare di Dio* are very human: the actors are very much flesh and blood. Francesco, always unobtrusive, is just another of the brothers (a happy idea that heightens the bias towards anonymity, used so successfully in *Paisà*). He weeps like a child both after kissing the leper and when the time comes to leave his companions. Brother Ginepro wears an unchanging, happy expression which can initially appear stupid but ultimately becomes moving. Brother Giovanni, the oldest member of the community, has the sturdy look of a rustic, his features etched by time, and speaks only with difficulty. All the faces reveal enough emotional fervour within to make us fellow-creatures of these unknown men, lost in time, and to bring the Franciscan spirit of the past to the present. Thirteen years later, Pier Paolo Pasolini was to be the first to take advantage of this lesson in reliving an emotion which has already been lived by showing comparable intuition (although specifically in terms of a whole pictorial school) in his extempore choosing of actors for *Il Vangelo secondo Matteo*.

These actions and faces that allow the rediscovery of a historical age, the feeling of period. The conventional, *ad hoc* 'creation of atmosphere' in historical films has been whittled down in *Francesco, giullare di Dio* simply to ideas: Nicolaio's castle becomes no more than a camp; towns are hardly seen or viewed from afar; the clothes are completely timeless. An attempt, then, is made to recapture the period, not in the conventional way with décor, but through actions caught, as if accidentally, by the camera, without any judgement being made. A rider kills a man who intended to rob him; immediately he gives alms to Francesco, a witness to the murder, who cannot hold back his tears. Ginepro is dragged, with quite needless cruelty, around the camp and almost has his head chopped off. (Nicolaio surveys the friar with the same amazement as that with which Major Bergmann in *Roma, città aperta* examines Don Pietro.) A few brief indications satisfactorily convey the prevalent climate of violence in mediaeval Italy. The figure of Nicolaio is amazing in this respect: encased in armour so heavy that he cannot stir, he regards Ginepro's humility (which he finds completely abnormal) with all the fear and mistrust of a prehistoric tribal chief confronted by the spells of a witch doctor. His terror is shown in puppet-like movements. It would be impossible to find a more tersely apposite image for the obtuse mentality if feudal overlords. And it would be no less impossible to find a more genuine expression of the spiritual vitality, absurdity, even delirium of the thirteenth-century Franciscans than in the unbelievable sight (which belongs to the realms of fantasy) of Brother Ginepro running down the hill in front of a giant barrel, which follows him like a little dog and which he was going to use in the preparation of a fortnight's provisions. And again there is the image of Ginepro in his humility, filling a glass with blood from his nose after the blows he suffers at the encampment.

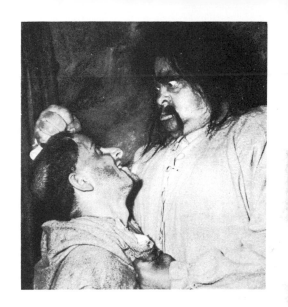

Francesco giullare di Dio can rightly be regarded as the first *true* historical film, in which time is abolished so that a distant past can be examined 'in the present'. This process was applied to the recent past in *Roma, città aperta* and, particularly, *Paisà* (from which the monastery episode set in Romagna clearly helped inspire *Francesco giullare di Dio*) where it managed to turn chronicle into history. Here, history (or, if you like, legend) becomes chronicle. This approach remains an essential of Rossellini's work and foreshadows his films for television. The extreme economy of the chronicle gives it an eternal quality: the Franciscan message is entirely relevant to the present and the little brothers of St. Francis remain alive forever.

Its prodigiously natural quality makes *Francesco, giullare di Dio* as much of an exemplary film as *Paisà* (from which its episodic structure is derived) and a uniquely successful one. It can either attract or repel, depending on the feelings of the audience about the religion celebrated by the film. (One could even adopt the position of the enraged pig-owner pursued by Brother Ginepro who mumbles excuses and offers his own foot – but doubtless one would be pursuing such a hostile attitude to no avail because the film can disarm anyone with its coherence, in the same way as the peasant was disarmed into giving the brothers the whole animal.) Paradoxically, *Francesco, giullare di Dio* seems at once a very simple film and very complex, very religious and very materialistic, very wise and absolutely raving. Although it is a work of perfect harmony, it remains a real artistic challenge.

Europa '51

Irene Girard is living a frivolous life, when her child, Michele, thinking that she has lost interest in him, commits suicide. In her grief, she turns for comfort to her cousin Andrea, a militant communist, who advises her to work for the material good of others. She goes into the slums, makes new friends and even does a day's work in a factory in place of a woman who is in need. Disappointed by this experience of activism, she turns to giving spiritual help. After caring devotedly for a sick prostitute, Irene helps a young delinquent to escape and comes to the attention of the police. Her husband sends her to be examined by psychiatrists at a clinic. Here, because she stubbornly insists that her acts are the result of moral demands and not of temporary insanity, she will be confined permanently.

Apart from her curious refusal to take the Rorschach test, while she is at the psychiatric clinic, Irene Girard appears to be a perfectly normal woman. The electroencephalogram shows nothing wrong, and she reacts just as normally to the tachystoscope, with its flashing light very much like a flickering film projector. If the camera is unable to reach the secrets hidden behind a face (a topic dealt with – and how – by Godard), the apparatus of science is just as incapable of distinguishing spiritual processes. Although we are dealing with an individual case history, the film revolves around a character who is in full possession of her mental faculties. 'I have not lost my mind', Irene declares to her mother-in-law, when she goes home after her visit to the slum.

Irene displays a state of Perfect Charity, in so extreme a way as to appear abnormal, when she helps a sick prostitute and a young delinquent, when she does a day's work in a factory for a friend. The common bourgeois reflex of regarding anything out of the ordinary as a misdemeanour causes the others to greet Irene's activities with hostility, the more so because her self-sacrifice indicts their own egotism. In their eyes, Irene is as much strange as unbalanced, just as she appears to the women in the asylum, who surround her like spiders (or like the idiots in the village closing in on the poor country girl in *Il miracolo*). Of course, you do not expect to see a rich *bourgeoise* going to take the place of an extremely humble woman in her grindingly hard work at a factory. But such an unusual act is only a symptom of the extreme moral upheaval which, if we are to believe the director, appeared frequently in Italy after the war. There is an important antecedent for this in the secular experience of Simone Weil (on which, here, is superimposed the religious experience of St Francis of Assisi).

In any case, the audience is not encouraged to identify with the character's point of view. After the drowning of a little boy, Irene visits the district in which he lived. This is shown in a long panning shot which ends on her contemplating it. Although we discover things with her, no attempt is made to force us to share her ideas. We are asked to believe, not in a world where transcendent values exist, but in people to whom these values are revealed – an entirely different matter. Irene's actions are significant in expressing feelings characteristic of a period in time, which the director has tried to capture at all costs *in the present* and has indicated even in the film's title.

When Irene says good-bye to her cousin, Andrea, her face is divided equally between light and shade (the previous scene of her painful discussion with her husband had her completely hidden in shadow). Irene's confusion is taken into account visually as well as conceptually. Until the death of her son, Michele, she has never looked at the world. Now she confronts life, pain (the drowned boy, the dying prostitute), love (the little girl who asks for a kiss, the happiness of the servant with her children and friends), work (the factory). In taking upon herself the pain and the travail of others – the death of the prostitute, the affair of the young delinquent, the factory woman's work, and so on – Irene finds that she has great resources of love, still fresh and unreleased, which have to overflow on someone or something. This love, which seems incomprehensible in terms of the external factors, seems so limitless that it finally reaches the level of Perfect Charity. Its generating force is made clear with great sensitivity when Irene holds the epileptic woman in the same position as that in which she embraces her son to comfort him in the moments before his death.

Europa '51, like *L'amore* and *Stromboli, terra di Dio*, tends to become identified with the face of the star, and even the structure of the film assumes the confused, passionate nature of this image. The development is abrupt and jerky. There is no time wasted, no logical progression to justify the terse unfolding of the action, or to make it 'convincing'. The film is only a statement of the facts, but nonetheless implies an attitude that is, in some respects, a violent one. The factory Irene goes into looks like the bridge of a battleship, work is not shown as a worthy task, but as degrading labour. The priest at the clinic displays a complete inability to reason with Irene – in fact he seems moderately idiotic, bearing a strange resemblance to Fernandel. An attempt is made to express a far-reaching moral conflict, which is incarnated in a woman's face, merely by means of a series of actions, sketched out in a few strokes with a simplification that touches on abstraction.

Ultimately, it is this face that gives internal

Frames: Europa '51 – Michele; Irene with her son and her husband.

coherence to an otherwise notably discontinuous film, in the same way as the image of Falconetti or Anna Karina fills the gaps in *La Passion de Jeanne d'Arc* or *Vivre sa vie*. When Irene's face, imbued, as it is, with such strength, appears on the screen, the consequent depth of emotion makes us forget the quite short, but irritating explanatory passages. We can dismiss what is being put across in the film's description of the crisis – *Europa '51* becomes a real 'message picture' at times – the better to understand the sublimity of the woman's sacrifice. *Europa '51* is Rossellini's most paradoxical film; one has to look for its significance in its images rather than in its ideas. The film is an ascent from the darkness of the beginning, towards a dazzling light of the end, when Irene realises that in her whole, confused scale of values, established by an unrighteous society, the only certainty is her need to devote the whole of her great capacity for love to others. This certainty leads her to regain her inner freedom as if by chance through an unconscious development. It is quite astonishing how a film like this, passionate to the point of indecency, manages to advance steadfastly towards the extreme bareness of the conclusion, which is bathed in an unearthly, Nordic light and has an austerity worthy of Dreyer. No Mediterranean director can ever have come so close to achieving the spiritual quality of *Ordet*, which was to be shot three years after *Europa '51*.

The film carries the rejection of anecdote to its logical conclusion and dispenses with the glamour conferred on the previous films by their settings: the ruins of Germany, the desolate island of Stromboli, the simple beauty that nature holds for the Franciscans. But it is also the sum of these films: the hideous spiritual effect of war on a child from *Germania, anno zero*, the grim isolation of a woman in a universe that does not respond to her demands from

Stromboli, terra di Dio and the attainment of perfect charity from *Francesco, giullare di Dio*. Equally, it is clarified and extended by them. It is a generous and intolerant account of a troubled and confused period and of a strange reality that has to be captured and understood as quickly as possible. Finally, *Europa '51* makes it plain that Rossellini, is not trying to create an *oeuvre* composed of several self-contained films, but use a series of film fragments to create a single, composite film.

Frames: Europa '51 – *Ingrid Bergman as Irene.*

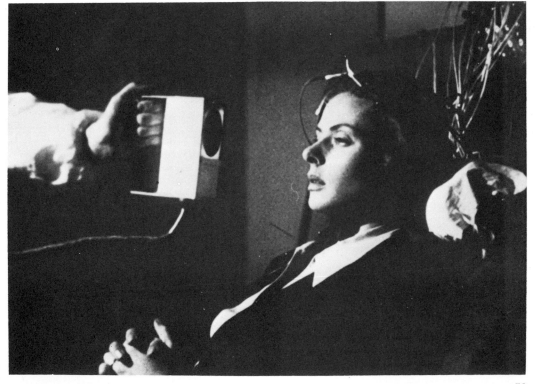

Dov'è la libertà?

After twenty years in solitary confinement for killing his best friend (who was his wife's lover), Salvatore Locajono is pardoned and leaves prison. He is released on New Year's Eve and seeks shelter successively, with a troupe of dancers, in a poor district where he works as a barber (until the truth about his past gets out), and finally with his wife's family. One day he learns that the girl he loves is pregnant by someone else. Salvatore is overwhelmed by this new disappointment and decides to go back to prison, the only place where he has been happy. He sneaks back to his cell in the night. Accused of 'invasion of a public building', he is convicted and returns happily to prison.

Paradox is the predominant quality in *Dov'è la libertà?* The closed world of the prison seems pleasant and friendly ('*un bello castello*', where the password is '*tutti per uno, uno per tutti*', as the unfortunate Salvatore explains to the court) while the world outside is cruel, absurd and egotistical. Salvatore is thrown out of his new home when he is found to be an ex-convict. An 'old friend' uses him to pass a false bank-note in buying powdered milk. He is called delinquent by the warder who finds him in his old cell (then this representative of the law starts whining 'I am a man with a family . . .'). Salvatore had yelled exactly the same accusation at his 'old friend' when he learned about the swindle. He can get back to prison only by stealing the governor's coat, in order to look like him . . . In post-war Italy, everything is relative; values are all confused.

The hat given to Salvatore on his release is too big for him. It is an early warning of the inadequacy of the external world. Outside, he appears ill at ease with urban life. Without any firm intention, he buries his face in the enormous bosom of a girl he has never seen before – the same gag appears ten years later in Jerry Lewis's *The Nutty Professor*. He is followed down the street by a herd of cows, like Buster Keaton in *Go West* (1926). Salvatore has no better luck with people. The dancers take no notice of him, his landlady does not trust him, and his wife's relatives humiliate him deeply. The story is about the impossibility of adapting to the world after twenty years in prison, but there is nothing in his personality to make Salvatore a misfit. He can apply himself skilfully to his trade as a barber, both in prison and in the district where he tries to settle. He even displays ingenuity, for example in the dance competition where he stands in for the musicians who are on strike by whistling and humming the orchestral parts. Salvatore has quite a liking for women. He regards the dancer Aironne with a lecherous look when her breasts come close to his nose. He hums the same love song to Maria, the landlady's daughter, and to the young Agnese in his wife's family home. His weakness for women is highlighted by two heart-rending *plans-séquences*: 1) in prison, he weeps at the singing of another prisoner, whom he is shaving, after helping him to write a love-letter; 2) on New Year's Eve, alone in the street and just released from gaol, he cannot conceal his distress and tells his whole story to a girl he bumps into; he has been imprisoned for twenty years for killing the friend with whom his wife was unfaithful. He courts Maria, who does not think much of him, and then Agnese, only to discover in the end that she is pregnant by someone else.

Salvatore has a terrible fear of loneliness, but he cannot help seeing that he is being driven towards it. When his landlady learns that he is an ex-convict, he is thrown out of his lodgings. Then he sadly packs his case and opens one of the packets of powdered milk he bought with the forged money. Alone in a café near the end

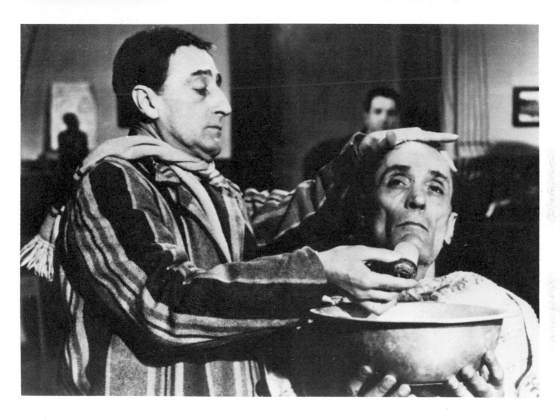

Still: Dov'è la libertà? – *Totò as Salvatore.*

of the film, the unfortunate man enviously observes the happy situation of the prison governor, who can return whenever he likes to Salvatore's former home. He is conscious of his predicament only at certain moments, when his movements betray his loneliness with an intensity of feeling that banishes the melodrama to which the film is always close. (Here we see to full advantage the tragi-comic talent that Totò did not have the chance to use again until thirteen years later in Pasolini's *Uccellacci e uccellini*.)

Salvatore's desire to return to prison, where

he was happy, comes as a logical consequence. Finally, in the café he has his inspiration of stealing the prison governor's hat and coat. This opens every door for him until he is in his old cell and can go to sleep with a happy smile. *Dove'è la libertà?* again raises the problem of freedom and at the same time displays some surprising affinities with *Europa '51*, which was shot in the same year. Both films have a similar outcome, the same meaning, and their subjects are very akin to one another. *Dov'è la libertà?*

is the perfect corollary to *Europa '51*. It serves, above all, to elaborate on *Europa '51*, which builds up a coherent, complex argument. It is precisely the differences between the two films that add to the significance of *Europa '51*. *Dov'è la libertà?* tells a related story with rather different shades of meaning. Where Irene is moved by charity, Salvatore acts out of selfishness. He appoints himself spokesman for order and morality. He is shocked to learn that, while he has been in prison, his wife has been the mistress of a Jew, Torquatti, whom he meets again at her family home. The man had been interned during the war in a German concentration camp; even so, Salvatore complains that the family is mixing with a deportee. He gives up the idea of marrying Agnese because she is expecting a baby. Salvatore has built up his own little happiness shut up in prison for twenty years, while outside there took place the triumph and fall of Fascism, the tragedy of war

Stills: Dov'è la libertà? − *Salvatore Locajono tries to find happiness out of prison.*

and the dramas of peace. His whole idea of happiness is based on illusion, pure and simple. Throughout the film he shows a completely *petit bourgeois* spirit, just like that of the community which rejects him (*Dov'è la libertà?* is a great deal more vaguely placed in history than *Europa '51*, but some of its details clearly place the story at the time when the film was shot − again it is extremely faithful to current reality.)

The contrasting characters of Irene and Salvatore also determine the differences in the construction between the films. *Europa '51* is a simple statement of facts; *Dov'è la libertà?* takes the form of a philosophical fable. Its less rigorous construction can be put down to accidental reasons: the sequences of Salvatore's trial were filmed after the rest of the shooting, and not by Rossellini. The part of the story that takes place in the present was thus broken up into a series of flashbacks – a procedure which is the exact antithesis of Rossellini's. (In this respect, we can imagine that Rossellini's version would have begun on Salvatore before his release, fully immersed in prison life.) But the problem is still put in the same way: freedom can only be found in a knowledge of oneself. Irene and Salvatore achieve this by different routes; if she reaches a state that is super-human, almost saintly, he remains entirely human. He is shabby and luckless, too close to us and too like us for comfort.

Viaggio in Italia

Alexander and Katherine Joyce, a quiet English couple, arrive in Naples by car; they have come to find a buyer for property left to them by a relative. They settle in with a friend, Burton, and his wife. While Katherine goes sightseeing in the town and the surrounding neighbourhood, Alexander is discreetly bored. Both become jealous, mainly because, for the first time in their marriage, they lack the protective screen of business and social events in London. After a futile row, Alexander decides to get a divorce. But at a religious occurrence they are swept along by the crowd and realise the need they both have for each other.

Viaggio in Italia opens with the view down a road, seen through the windscreen of a car and then through a side window. The film's raw material is the world and reality. This rather long-held image of reality, consisting of two shots, lasting fifteen seconds and ten seconds, followed by the image of the Joyces asleep – one shot lasting twenty-two seconds – give a curious feeling of continuance, as if the film had begun a lot earlier. We are not present at the opening of a story, merely coming in on something that was already going on, as we do in real life. *Viaggio in Italia* is also a film about time and duration.

The subsequent shots give a superficial but realistic picture of the Joyces, an English couple on holiday in Italy. They exchange common-place remarks from which we learn that a) Alexander is bored – 'In this country noise and boredom go together perfectly', b) they have come to Italy to sell a house left them by an uncle and c) they have never spent so much time alone together in the whole of their married life. The arrangement of these shots also indicates to us; 1) the surprise that this strange country, the new scenery and a different reality arouse in Katherine (a succession of intercut shots, alternately objective and subjective); 2) the lack of intimacy between husband and wife (seen in setting, position and tempo); 3) the automatic reactions which typically betray the English abroad – Katherine cleans a squashed insect off the windscreen and asks if there is any danger of catching malaria, Alexander criticises the way Italians drive and so on. The way in which these observations are set out displays an aloof and acid humour, new to Rossellini's films.

Viaggio in Italia takes as its subject the break-up of a marriage, but it is not a tragedy. It is about a reconciliation, but is not a comedy. It revolves around Italy, but is not a documentary. Indeed, it does not fit into any of the conventional classifications. As a film about reality and time, it comes into the sphere of the essay. This explains some of the things which struck both audience and critics at the time: the absence of dramatic construction (almost nothing happens – the characters stroll around museums, gaze out to sea, admire the landscape and attend social functions), the abrupt development of the action (a sudden, silly quarrel ends in the decision to get a divorce and the solution to the conflict occurs suddenly and unexpectedly), the unbalanced composition of shots and the actors' flat delivery of their lines.

The weight of these objections seems debatable, considering that nothing much is likely to happen to an English couple on holiday abroad. It does not need Alexander to become the lover of an exiled Russian countess in Capri, or Katherine to have an affair with the head of the Mafia in Naples to bring about their divorce. The action, therefore, is systematically founded on quiet periods, that is to say, on the normal rhythm of tourist life – commonplace conversations, meals, the siesta, social gatherings, sightseeing trips, and so on. All this satisfies the demands of direct, external realism but is not unimportant from the dramatic point of view. The drowsy chats on the terrace during their siesta, references to the young poet who has been Katherine's lover, and Alexander's sarcasm all add up to an explicit picture of their psychological state and their relationship. The meals at the villa where they suffer the ritual consumption of spaghetti make clear their embarrassment when faced with, to them, unfamiliar customs. They are also confronted with the love of their host and hostess, which brings home to them the picture of their own love. Their outings bring into the open jealous or spiteful reactions which at first are surprising in such peaceful English people – the meeting in the restaurant arouses a jealous outburst from Katherine at Alexander's attentiveness to other women. And at the party given by the Duke of Lipoli, it is Alexander's turn to get jealous at his wife's dazzling social success. The sightseeing trips themselves form less of a travelogue than a mirror reflecting the reactions of Alexander and Katherine to their surroundings, the discoveries they make about themselves.

Sightseeing trips play a fairly large part in this film about two tourists. At first sight, the visit to the Archaeological Museum at Capodimonte in Naples seems to fall into the usual pattern. They look at things quickly and superficially; the guide has a Neapolitan accent and an off-colour sense of humour – an amusing caricature of the typical Italian guide. Showing them a group of dancers he remarks 'The fourth is the image of my daughter Mariannina', and in front of Hercules leaning on his club, he exclaims 'God, everyone here is resting except me.' But the visit is shown from a highly unusual angle. The figures of dancers, satyrs, fauns, discus throwers and the rest are filmed with the pans and tracking shots that have become the hallowed conventions of art documentaries. But here the movements always end on Katherine, the subject who is looking. The approach has nothing to do with art documentary; it remains objective and, above all, forms a summary of a woman's reactions – her lips, puritanically pursed at the statue of a satyr, give the feeling of Katherine's surprise at this

Still: Viaggio in Italia – *Katherine (Ingrid Bergman) goes sightseeing.*

outburst of life and sensual joy emanating from the stone of these groups. The crane movement up over Hercules's shoulders to look down at Katherine standing at the base, dwarfed by the statue, is not merely to give a beautiful ending to a fine piece of film, but is a visual statement of the relationship between two completely different civilisations. It is in this that true significance and originality of this sequence lies.

From the start of their confrontation with

Italy, the Joyces come under the influence of its scenery, climate, food and social customs; these imperceptibly effect a real change in their relationship with each other. Katherine, who is the more receptive, is consequently the more affected. The sea, the sun, other women's attraction to Alexander and the love that their hosts Tony and Natalie Burton have for each other, awaken in her an unexpected romanticism (which materialises in the recollection of her former lover, the poet Charles Lewington) coupled with a compelling need to torment her husband. Since she is constantly fascinated by life (pregnant women, babies, the sensual presence of the statues) and death (the burial, and the catacombs in the Fontanelle church) all the little things that happen, all the images that she absorbs during her stay gradually combine to make a deep impression upon her, releasing aspects of her personality that she has been trying to ignore. We are always shown reality from Katherine's point of view just as we were from Karin's in *Stromboli, terra di Dio* or Irene's in *Europa '51*. But this viewpoint, achieved by means of conventional intercutting, does not put across a subjective feeling or encourage identification by the audience. *Viaggio in Italia* uses the *contrechamp* with great originality, not to give a subjective view of the character's field of vision (a principle upon which Hitchcock has based a whole dialectic), but as the objective picture of a piece of reality which is at that time affecting the character. In this sense the film is the culmination of an effort started in *Germania, anno zero* to show how environment can work imperceptibly on a human being.

Alexander, too, is affected by his surroundings, but in a different way. Paying less attention than his wife to the surroundings, he keeps his distance and does not allow the spectacle of Italian life to make an impression on him. On the other hand, he remains very sensitive to human relationships, through which he makes an effort to increase his personal standing. But he fails in his attempts to start an affair with Marie and later with the prostitute whom he meets by chance (a scene which foreshadows Sandro's encounter with the whore in *L'Avventura*). Here there is none of the intercutting which goes with Katherine. The vehicle for expressing his relationships with the two women is the *plan-séquence*. He pretends to remain unmoved, but at his first disagreement with his wife – Katherine has left him without the car – he decides to get a divorce, a solution which is quite out of proportion to the importance of the dispute. Jealousy, the quarrel between the engaged couple (which he overhears at his window, in the half-light, and is unexpectedly disturbed by) and Marie's difficulties with her husband, all bring him back with a jolt to the thought of his own problem. In a different way to his wife, he too suffers from the hostile reality around him.

It is the unimportant events that play silently on the Joyces. Their involvement with their problem becomes so close that it breaks up from time to time into strikingly violent ellipses. After the visit to the Capodimonte museum, Katherine confesses to Alexander her disgust at the immodesty of the statues, which we have already been shown in her grimace at the satyr. Alexander is jealous of the hit his wife scored the night before at the party given by the Duke of Lipoli and tells her that he is going off to Capri 'to enjoy himself'. Katherine cannot hide her resentment and loudly expresses her disgust on a car trip across Naples. So in the temple of Sibilla Cumana, when she is grabbed by the guide to show how the Turks tied up their prisoners – 'a beautiful woman like you would have been tied up like this' – she brushes him off furiously and leaves in the direction of the temple of Apollo, muttering 'All men are the same! Cynical and cruel!' This interaction within *Viaggio in Italia* sometimes takes on a complexity that defies attempts at analysis.

The pressure of reality on the Joyces is especially insistent in the visit to the ruins of Pompeii at the end of the film. They are deeply moved and even Alexander is sufficiently shaken out of his attitude of detachment to admit the impression made on him by the sight of two bodies which have just been uncovered, petrified in an eternal embrace. This couple,

Still: Viaggio in Italia – *Katherine and Alexander (George Sanders) visit Pompeii.*

preserved in a gesture of perfect love, reflect a cruel picture of the Joyces' situation, with the futility and bitterness of parting. But also, they represent a civilisation whose harmony, unlike that of the Joyces, is irrevocably lost. (Ten years later, Godard based *Le Mépris* on this theme, and makes a direct reference in it to *Viaggio in Italia*.) This idea is stressed by desperate flight through a setting of serene and peaceful ruins. Their flight, which neither of them tries to conceal, is the warning of a crisis. This comes at the procession, when they are separated in the crowd of people excited by the noise of

a miracle. Attempts have been made to see the miracle as an external echo of the internal miracle taking place inside them. The rashness of this interpretation becomes clear from the lack of evidence of the miracle. We see only a man waving his crutches in the air. The importance of this moment for the Joyces lies in the change of reality from being a factor which works on them subjectively, into something objective and active. It intervenes, separating them to reveal their isolation and their mutual need by breaking down their emotional barriers. By provoking their reunion, reality absorbs into itself, regaining the primacy it had at the start of the film. The end of *Viaggio in Italia* centres on the crowd and anonymity. The last shot (which is missing from many copies) lingers on the players in a band, a non-significant image, if ever there was one. The dénouement of *Viaggio in Italia* remains quite ambiguous. For a moment, the Joyces become aware of emotions they would like to hide at any price, and once again feel the need to take refuge in each other. For how long? Like the question of Karin's future at the end of *Stromboli, terra di Dio*, there is only one answer – that would be another film.

At this stage, it may seem surprising to uncover such a complex drama beneath some banal dialogue and a few aimless trips. But, like *Paisà*, this apparently disjointed and haphazard film is organised with the utmost discipline. The shots could almost be improvised, but each has a definite purpose in the film as a whole. The *plan-séquence* in the Florentine episode of *Paisà*, where Harriet and Massimo walk down the steps of a block of flats among anxious tenants, allows, with a remarkable feeling for synthesis, a) the individual to be shown in the midst of the group, b) the characters to remain unseparated from their environment, c) an event to last the actual time it takes. When the Joyces reach Naples, we follow in long continuous panning shots the arrival of their car at the hotel entrance, and then their progress from the entrance to the lift door. The principle which applied, in *Paisà*, to actions which were dramatic in themselves, here is used in the presentation of trivial, everyday acts. The characters' confrontation with reality and themselves is shown with *champs-contrechamps* which nevertheless respect the logical continuity of the action. *Viaggio in Italia* tends towards the overall feeling of a very long *plan-séquence*.

This idea of continuity is extremely important when it comes to reaching one of the possible levels on which the film has meaning. The feeling of constant movement by the camera as it tirelessly pursues the characters is not there with an eye to the beauty of the image, but to express their movements and contribute to the general rhythm of the shots. When a character moves, the composition of the shot is unbalanced. The balance is at once restored, but straight away is called into question by further movement by a character. The unceasing search for equilibrium and the recognition of its transience constitute the subject of *Viaggio in Italia*. But the importance of the idea of continuity lies most of all in the concern for *duration*, which is without doubt the film's most novel and significant quality. The *plans-séquence* are very long, though they do not extend time as Antonioni, for example, was to do later, but their choice and position in the film contribute greatly to the synthesis. Nevertheless, they give a feeling of length, particularly as they portray actions which are not in themselves dramatic. In spite of appearances, *Viaggio in Italia* is quite the reverse of a slow film. As the entire action barely covers five days, in this sense it is unbelievably speedy. And although the takes are, on average, long, sequences are joined abruptly with brutal juxtapositions, as in the interaction of the scenes leading up to Katherine's outburst at the Temple of Apollo. There are others with an economy of effects and richness of information that give them the same spirit of synthetical invention as *October*. Katherine's arrival at the Capodimonte museum is very succintly handled in a panning shot along the foot of a pillar to the sound of a Neapolitan song. Some of these ideas of *mise-en-scène* have an abstract beauty reminiscent of the stylisation of Matisse, whose influence on the level of rhythm and composition is obvious here. Godard was later indirectly to acknowledge this philosophy of the cinema: 'In *Made in USA* there is a book

jacket on which can be read *Gauche, année zéro*. The last time this caption appears, the beginning of a movement of Schumann's Fourth Symphony is heard. Unless you're blind and deaf, it's impossible not to see that this shot, this mixture of image and sound, represents a movement of hope. You can call it false, ridiculous, childish, provocative, but it is what it is, like a scientific object.'

The 'mixture of image and sound' is in itself

Still: Viaggio in Italia – *the final sequence; Alexander and Katherine in the crowd.*

enough to destroy the legend of improvisation, at least in the normal sense, as applied to this film, as to all Rossellini's other films. It is enough to make clear the effort of stripping down to essentials which is the culmination of the efforts made in one way in *Paisà*, and in another in *Germania, anno zero*, *Stromboli, terra di Dio* and *Europa '51*. Conscious rejection of the usual dramatic conventions in an increasingly close (and increasingly questioning) adherence to reality has surprisingly led a director who has not so far been exactly famous for his story-telling, to invent a new idea of cinematic duration and realism. Underlying the film there is a strange fire, similar in kind to the ionisation at Campi Flegrei which so fascinates Katherine. The film is as much about the universe as *Stromboli, terra di Dio*, in that it is dependent on the basic elements of earth, water and fire. *Viaggio in Italia*, which you might think of as *Italia, terra di Dio*, manages to incorporate in one work a wide range of experience. It is an autobiographical film, a home movie in which a man talks about himself, his wife, his friends and the country in which he lives. It is a dynamic and sleepy film, which entirely fulfils the author's own thoughts on the nature of the cinema. It is a film essay on the feelings of men today, with a moral bearing rare in the cinema. It is a private notebook complaining, before the event, of the complete alienation of our civilisation. It is . . . But it is enough to say that, while *Paisà* in 1946 raised a new standard of realism in the cinema, only seven years later, *Viaggio in Italia* imposed another, the ethical and aesthetic requirements of which provide perhaps the most important precedent in modern cinema. Jacques Rivette was right when he stated in Cahiers du Cinéma 45 in what is still the finest article written on Rossellini, that 'on the appearance of *Viaggio in Italia* all other films suddenly aged ten years.' Today it is still an *avant-garde* film.

Three Sketches

L'Invidia (*in* Les Sept Péchés Capitaux). *A painter, Orfeo, marries Camille. She discovers that he spends most of his time with a cat, which he has had for a long time. Camille is jealous and kills the animal.*

Ingrid Bergman (*in* Siamo donne). *Signora Rossellini, doing her housework, is irritated by a hen which is pecking at her roses. She shuts the villain up and tries to make her dog, Locajono, devour it. But Signora Annovacci, the owner of the bird, arrives in time to save it.*

Napoli '43 (*in* Amori di mezzo secolo). *A chorus girl, Carla, gets to know Renato, a soldier on leave, during a pause in the bombing of Naples. They discover that they love each other but are killed in each other's arms by a bomb.*

Rossellini once said that '*Roma, città aperta* is a film about "fear": everyone's fear, but above all my own.' The intimate, personal side becomes increasingly apparent in his films from *Viaggio in Italia* – a filmed notebook on contemporary man and a real home movie, since its main components were the director's wife, his Jaguar, his villa and his domestic problems. The home movie side is stressed even more in the episodes shot after 1952. Freed from the dramatic requirements of a feature (even allowing for the liberties taken in that direction in the features from *Stromboli, terra di Dio* to *Viaggio in Italia*), a sketch can adopt a more direct approach to certain ideas and experiences.

L'Invidia takes as its subject a woman's relationship with a cat, *Ingrid Bergman* deals with that of another woman and a hen. The first woman is married to a painter, the second to a film director. The personal level at which the two films are pitched is obvious. Surprising

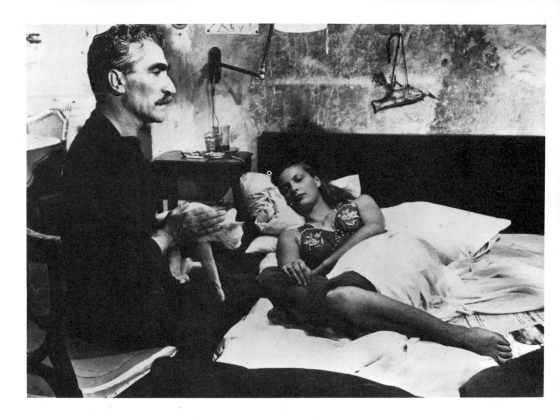

Still: L'Invidia – *Rossellini's sketch in* Les Sept Péchés Capitaux – *the painter, Orfeo, his cat and his envious wife, Camille.*

prominence is given to the conflict between man and other animals, towards which humans display a particularly murderous attitude. Camille kills the cat, Ingrid tries to make her dog eat the hen. This forms a strange contrast with the perfect harmony of man's relationship with animals proclaimed later in *India*.

The originality of *Ingrid Bergman* lies in its frank presentation as a home movie made by

the director having fun, filming his wife, his home, his children (little Robertino throws stones in the water and his brothers are playing with a pony), his dog (called Locajono like the leading character in *Dov'è la libertà?*), the gardener and the servants. These ingredients are used to produce the feeling of a realistic private joke, beginning with the actress's way of expressing herself. When she explains '*Le mie rose erano mature*', her neighbour drily retorts '*Mature si dice per frutti, non per fiori . . .*'

This observation is a fair statement of the purpose of the sketch, conceived as part of a

feature, built on an idea that was both quite ingenious and very silly – to reconstruct something of interest from the lives of four stars of the Italian cinema – the other three were Alida Valli, Isa Miranda and Anna Magnani – without any concern to show the more pleasant aspects of their characters. Whereas the other three episodes are made in the epic manner, in an attempt to construct a sort of inverted mythological pattern with its actresses, the approach here is marked by the most commonplace occurrences. Ingrid Bergman is shown as a housewife who struggles,

Still: Ingrid Bergman – *the star with Signora Annovacci and her hen.*

after a fashion, with the housework and engages in a futile battle with a hen, revealing a rather sadistic turn in her nature – she wants the dog to eat the hen alive. This rather disrespectful picture might have shocked audiences in Italy, and did, but for Anglo-Saxons who still regard Ingrid Bergman as one of the great Hollywood stars, it merely heightens the provocativeness to see her with this lack of warmth towards animals.

But this little story would not rise above the level of a charming private joke, if it did not raise the possibility of a different outlook. The narration follows the other episodes, being in the first person for the first time ever in a Rossellini film. After some holding back, Ingrid Bergman addresses the audience herself to tell the story. But her tale also has an objective detachment and describes, with the spontaneity typical of *Paisà* and *Francesco, giullare di Dio*, the trials of being a housewife. It is about how to talk to the gardener, confront a crabby neighbour, solve an annoying problem, how to look after the children at home and how to receive friends. The absolutely documentary seriousness with which this tiny domestic drama is handled makes the comedy of the ending even more delirious, with Bergman offering drinks to friends who have just arrived, while trying to stifle the despairing cries of the hen which she has shut in a cupboard in the dining room. The bird is finally saved by the arrival of Signora Annovacci. The episode shows a new standard of realism in filming such a situation. '*Ho detto che c'era una storia ridicola!*' cries the actress at the end as she leaves the audience. This ridiculous story – and *Viaggio in Italia*, made earlier the same year, is also a ridiculous story – is therefore only an excuse for further consideration of the idea of realism in the cinema. This little film also looks now like the illustrious ancestor of Godard's sketches from *Charlotte et son Jules* to *Le Grand Escroc*, which were inspired by a dialectic that is similar in all respects.

Napoli '43 could be an extra episode for *Paisà*: two young people who are soon to die find a fleeting moment of love. Moreover, the ending is that of *Paisà* when a bleak voice announces that the war ended three months later. But by 1954 the war was already a long way off and the chorus girl's encounter with the soldier lacks the immediacy of the GI's meeting with the Sicilian girl at the beginning of *Paisà*. It all seems to have been sifted by memory and is as far removed as a dream.

The starting point is still a strictly realistic account of the bombing, with wailing sirens, people crowded into a shelter praying, a girl with an injured leg, children crying, conversations in Neapolitan dialect. But a few details are all that is needed to give the whole story a look of fantasy. Carla, the chorus girl, is dressed like a mediaeval lady with a fine costume, all white. Her trembling movements and the emotion of her meeting with Renato, who was wounded in Sicily and is in action again after four months' convalescence, correspond to a whole tradition of courtly love. As they walk away from the shelter, the lovers look as if they were filmed in slow motion, although this is not the case. An immensely long tracking shot reveals the point of the story: two young people succeed in finding freedom, however briefly, in the midst of war. For once in Rossellini's films dream is confused with reality when the bomb unites the lovers eternally, though there is still a despairing 'Why?'.

Rossellini's first film in colour, *Napoli '43* is a quiet variation on several well-loved themes, a bitter-sweet, rather distant evocation – in a way his *Les visiteurs du soir*. This episode again combines technical experiment on the possibilities of colour and stylistic experiment on the lyrical re-examination of the past. This will be explored only once more, in *Giovanna d'Arco al rogo* – all the later experiments with the past, from *Viva l'Italia* to *Atti degli apostoli* are put as a consideration of history.

Despite Rossellini's polite compliance with the conventions decided on in each film, then, his episodes are strikingly consistent with the rest of his work. They prove his gift for the concise outline and – particularly in *Ingrid Bergman* – appear as bold and innovatory as his features.

Giovanna d'Arco al rogo

Joan of Arc looks down from heaven at her martyrdom on earth. With her confessor, Brother Domenico, she examines the circumstances and motives which led her to the stake and raised her to celestial grace.

By 1954, some of Rossellini's films, notably *Roma, città aperta* and *Paisà*, were already considered as classics, at least in France. In the circumstances, the most surprising quality of *Giovanna d'Arco al rogo* is its lack of pretension. The director hid behind his star, Ingrid Bergman, to mount a theatrical production which had no close connection with his film work or his usual preoccupations. In filming it, he does not claim to translate stage action into cinema, but humbly contents himself with recording the production. *Giovanna d'Arco al rogo* is a film souvenir of the production of Paul Claudel's oratorio '*Jeanne au bûcher*', with his wife in the title role, and must be regarded as the director's tribute to his favourite actress (and thus, in a way, as a continuation of *L'Amore*).

As she pauses between heaven and earth, Joan is summoned by Brother Domenico, who invites her to take another look at her trial, to review her whole passion up to her death at the stake. Everything that is shown we therefore see from Joan's point of view: the court, the card game, the children playing, the feast in the country which leads up to the king's coronation. This feeling cannot be achieved in the theatre without complicated effects involving sets or lighting. But it is to hand in the cinema simply with intercutting, which can isolate a character from its surroundings. The editing allows Joan to be kept separate from the visible world,

whereas on stage she would be confined there. All the events which we see through Joan's eyes derive their whole meaning in this way, which is only implicit in the text, a flat and mediocre rendering of mediaeval plays. The solution adopted here by the director is simple, but appropriate and dramatically effective. It is also quite consistent with Rossellini's ideas on theatrical creation: 'It is a simple job of arrangement, of making clear what is in the text.'

The interest of the film does not lie in what surrounds Joan – the mechanism in which she is caught – but in Joan herself. The director's intentions become clear if you compare his direction of Ingrid Bergman with that of Victor Fleming in *Joan of Arc* (1948). The latter has her as a rather athletic young girl who is a keen hand with the sword. But here Bergman remains very much flesh and blood, like all Rossellini's heroes and saints. Her voice, her tears and her joy are entirely human: she is celebrated as a woman – you can even see her breasts through the tunic. This making of Joan into flesh and blood brings alive her desire for freedom, for escape from the earthly prison which surrounds her and is described throughout the film in circular images enclosing her. She leaves them to join in a ring of little girls, a touching memory of her childhood freedom, but she will have to break away again in order to enter the divine circle. (Ancient mythology uses a circle as the symbol of heaven and of perfection.)

However, the concept of space that the film puts forward gains greater complexity. At the opening of *Giovanna d'Arco*, the camera moves in circles, exploring a world taking shape through mist until a hole (another circle) appears in the clouds and we see a high-angle shot of people forming a ring around Joan. Then we see the stake encircled by flames and finally empty, with the fire burnt out. This

Photograph: Rossellini in the theatre – his production of 'Jeanne au bûcher' *which toured Europe (here at the Stockholm Opera).*

rather cunning change might, without too much fear of exaggeration, be identified with the viewpoint of God. We therefore come to the tempting theory that the whole film is only the point of view on a point of view. In other words, we see things on earth through the eyes of Joan, who is seen in turn from the viewpoint of God. Of course, I am not offering this as a fact but merely as a tentative interpretation. At the end, through the same break in the clouds, we follow Joan's ascent to heaven in the form of pure light, which seems to bear out the cyclical structure.

The idea of the circle recurs at all levels in the film, in a) the dramatic construction, which ends where it began, b) the visuals, with all their circular forms, c) space, constantly closed in on itself, like a cyclorama which includes the whole set, and d) finally, the camera-movements characterised by pans and circular tracking shots which sooner or later are completed to close the circle. *Giovanna d'Arco al rogo*, though seeming static, is in fact an enormous slow gyration, gradually travelling round to return to its start. This cyclical structure, identifiable with the idea of prison is broken only at the end, with the fall of the chains that bind Joan to the stake. The prison has broken and the circle opens out into a line with Joan's ascent – her escape from the confines of the world. She is seen as a light through the hole in the clouds – as if sharing God's vantage point – then in her human form. The two points of view merge and the film comes to an end.

It has been asserted by Mario Verdone that this film has no connection with the cinema. On the contrary: it is a meditation on space, movement and time, a meditation on the cinema, and as such the most beautiful gift a film director could offer his wife.

Still: Giovanna d'Arco al rogo.

La Paura

Irene is the wife of an important German scientist, Albert Wagner. Without much involvement, she is having an affair with a composer and is stricken with remorse. A young woman, Joanna Schultze, blackmails her and Irene is frightened into giving her some money. Forced by her husband's attitude to lie, and unable to find more money, Irene threatens to go and tell the whole truth to the police. Joanna then confesses that she has been acting at the instigation of Albert to make Irene reveal her unfaithfulness. Griefstricken, Irene considers suicide, but realising that her death would be a betrayal of her children, leaves her husband to find shelter in her love for them.

We hear a tremulous voice off-screen: 'I was deceiving my husband and I reproached myself for it', as a car is travelling through a town on a rainy night, passing a traffic policeman who takes on a weird appearance lit by a neon lamp. *La Paura* opens with anxiety and darkness.

The *leit-motiv* of shadow continues throughout the film. Irene – the same name as the main character in *Europa '51*, perhaps in an attempt to connect the two films – is asked by her lover, Enrico, if she loves him. Hidden in darkness, she replies 'I don't know'. She goes home and walks around in the dark until her husband appears and turns on the light in their bedroom. Later, when pressed by him, Irene has to invent a lie to explain the disappearance of the ring which Joanna has taken on account. All this time she remains in the shadow, visible only as a silhouette. Albert, too, is characterised by shadow. The last time we see him in the film, he is lurking in the shadows in front of the café where Joanna is talking with her victim.

The significance of this *leit-motiv* is defined by the contrast of the light, which pervades some moments in the film. Irene's escape from her anguish as she goes to see her children at the country house is revealed by a very long subjective tracking shot, comparable with the one that opens *Viaggio in Italia*, moving out of the darkness of the forest into the light of day. This tracking shot is repeated at the end of *La Paura*, and finds a corollary in the governess's words, 'Your children's smiles will light your way.' On the morning after her arrival in the country, Irene wakes relaxed, lit brightly for the first time in the film, in a bedroom filled with light. The redeeming power of light bursts out shatteringly in the dénouement. Having discovered Albert's 'disgraceful behaviour', Irene goes into her office (which is in shadow) and conceives the idea of suicide. She makes for the laboratory along a threateningly dark corridor, sections of which light up behind her, catching up at the exact moment when she is picking up some bottles, apparently looking for a poison. The light literally saves her from death.

The real subject of the film emerges through the *mise-en-scène*. It is not a question of analysing the feeling of fear, but the need to see clearly, to understand – a theme shared by most of Rossellini's films. The alterations made to the original work by Stefan Zweig also fulfil the director's intentions. Zweig's story was about a deceived husband, a prominent lawyer who was afraid of losing his frivolous, idle wife. The best way he could think of to win her back was employing a woman to blackmail her relentlessly by posing as the discarded mistress of the wife's lover. When the wife finally comes close to killing herself, her husband reveals what he has been doing. The wife regains the peace which she had lost through her fear of discovery. This dull, bourgeois melodrama, with its conformist content, is drastically altered and enriched in the film by changes in construction and characters. The suspense arbitrarily maintained in the novel is removed: from the outset it is

obvious that Albert knows the whole truth, as
we can conclude from the looks he gives his
wife when he arrives, when he is questioning
his little girl (to make her admit to hiding her
brother's gun), at the concert and finally during
the experiment on the guinea pig. (His character
curiously foreshadows that of Mark Rutland
in *Marnie* (1964), whom Hitchcock himself
described in the trailer as a 'hunter'. Albert
is seen in hunting dress, going to the country.

Still: La Paura (Die Angst) – *Albert and Irene
in the laboratory.*

The two sequences of experiments, centring
on Irene's fascinated gaze and the scarcely
concealed curiosity with which Albert observes
her, are important. The first suggests that
Albert's behaviour is an extension of his
professional attitude. The second, following the
revelation of his intrigue, confirms this im-

pression, through Albert's insistence on stressing that the guinea-pig has died without pain (recalling the Nazi theories voiced to little Edmund by the teacher in *Germania, anno zero*) and then, immediately after, his reference to Irene's ring. On the other hand, the husband's stratagem, the *raison d'être* of the novel, is revealed three quarters of the way through the action of the film (again a Hitchcock parallel, this time with *Vertigo*). Shortly after Irene has tried unsuccessfully to find Joanna again in a hotel and get back her ring, the young woman meets Albert at a crossroads, for fresh instructions. Irene only finds out the truth later, when she meets Joanna in a café. Worn out by the long suspense, she threatens to go to the police. Joanna breaks down and tells her the truth, while Albert waits outside in the shadows to hear the result of the latest move in his game.

Thus the character of Albert Wagner is presented in its true light. In treating his wife like a guinea-pig, he embodies a debased idea of science: its discipline is degraded by his failure to recognise individual rights. Albert forces his little girl to admit what she has done – clearly a warning to Irene, who remains in the middle of the frame throughout the interrogation – and punishes her afterwards to show that he will submit his wife to the same treatment in the name of a wrong-headed code of ethics. He loves Irene sincerely, and admires her for her courage, as she kept up the factory while he was a prisoner of war. However, these ethics, which led Edmund to kill his father, impel Albert to commit a spiritual crime and destroy the love of his wife. Contrary to Marcel Oms's accusation, the film does not advocate conformity. In *La Paura*, the Wagners have no reconciliation (although it may be that the producer who renamed it *Non credo più all'amore* for commercial distribution, also changed the order of the scenes to give a different impression, which in no way emerges from Rossellini's version), nor does the wife rush into her husband's arms imploring forgiveness.

Irene is fascinated by the animals injected with curare, but like a frightened guinea-pig, she, too, given away by her anxious, almost convulsive movements and her uncertain gestures. The way she opens the door and, without looking, puts down the money demanded by the blackmailer is significant here. She knows only one moment of relief from her nightmare. The long tracking shot taking her out of darkness into light *ends* when the car stops by her waiting children. Her decision to kill herself on learning of the total pointlessness of her suffering is not an attempt to expiate her wrong-doing, but the result of no longer believing in her husband's love or in any of the things which formed the centre of her life after the war. She has only the love of her children, and telephones them in the country to say good-bye. (Godard might have remembered this scene when he had Ferdinand ring home before his suicide in *Pierrot le Fou*.) This love will be her means of understanding the truth, the medium of which is light. She will emerge from the darkness into bright daylight to rejoin her children and forget the past.

La Paura is a disturbing account of both sides of a Germany that is at once both pastoral and technocratic, at the time of the economic miracle. In its return to contemporary Europe after Joan's ascent to heaven in *Giovanna d'Arco al rogo*, *La Paura* seems like a descent into hell. It could well be called *Viaggio in Germania* or *Germania, anno sette*, or even *Europa '54*, so completely does it confirm the constancy of the director's thought and inspiration. *La Paura* is a cool, northern film, almost Dreyer-like in contrast to the sensual warmth and erupting vitality of *Viaggio in Italia*. Significantly, it marked the end both professionally and maritally of Rossellini's partnership with Ingrid Bergman.

India

Some aspects of India in 1957 and 1958 are shown in four documentary episodes: 1) The marriage of a peasant and a pedlar's daughter in Kalepur, while elephants copulate. 2) A labourer bids farewell to the enormous dam at Hirakud, on which he has worked for five years. 3) The experience of an old man who tries to save a tiger from the huntsmen. 4) The travels of a monkey whose master has died of the heat. He is caught between the human world and the world of monkeys, until he finds a new owner.

After looking all round the gigantic installations of the dam at Hirakud, a humble workman does his ritual bathing at dusk in the artificial lake which his five long years of work have helped to create. Undoubtedly this is the finest shot in *India*, with a beauty that is not just the result of its plastic qualities: it is an ideal summary of the approach of the film as a whole in showing a fusion of the old and the new, of Man and Nature.

This latter theme takes on a special interest, as it has been prominent in Rossellini's earlier works, particularly *Viaggio in Italia*. It highlights the preoccupations of a director who was also bothered by the commercial failure of his films, by the lack of understanding encountered by his artistic ambitions and by the end of a whole stage in his personal life – the relationship with Ingrid Bergman. *India*, then, more than any other film by Rossellini, comes over as a renewed effort at research, a return to sources in a quest for fresh inspiration (or recaptured youth?) both away from European life and outside the dramatic conventions of his mortal enemy, the story film.

Like his very first documentaries, *India* is mainly devoted to animals. But there are no cobras or sacred cows: the elephant and the tiger are leading characters in the first and third of the four episodes, while the fourth has a monkey as its hero. We are not concerned only with animals, but with the relationship between animals and man – in which the director has already shown an interest, albeit from an entirely different angle, in *L'Invidia* and *Ingrid Bergman*. Here, the elephant, for instance, is the object of a religious ceremony in the holy town of Matura, but in the Kalepur jungle it is also employed to labour. Simultaneously a means of communicating with the deity and a partner in work, its duality is typical of hinduism. In a single long take, we see elephants coming to do their work. Their arrival is heralded by bells because, paradoxically, they are a real danger when their arrival is unannounced to passersby. From the wedding procession for the peasant and the pedlar's daughter – the completion of a short but detailed account of their betrothal, proposal of marriage, family intervention and so on – we cut sharply in a dazzling ellipsis to the pregnant elephant, ten months later. There is no humorous association; the point is to show as economically as possible that the lives of animals progress in parallel with those of men and that both are deeply rooted in Nature.

This first episode characterises the whole method of the film, based on resonances between shots and on abridgements in the narrative, which form a climax to the experiments in *Paisà* and *Viaggio in Italia*. Each shot in *India* gives rise to innumerable reverberations, which in turn inspire other shots, without ever moving from the original theme of the integration of Man and Nature. The story of the old man and the tiger rests on the essentials in the life of a man of eighty: prayers, morning ablutions, eating with his wife, teaching his sons, working with the oxen – a life, we discover, that is contemplative and regulated by a full acceptance of Nature. Into the midst of these everyday things, the old man's kind, careful dealings with a tiger introduce unexpected adventure and mystery. The arrival of prospectors' lorries in search of deposits of iron involves the intrusion of modernity (expressed in Philippe Arthuys' *musique concrète*) on the peace of country life, but it also signifies progress and the industry so necessary for the development of Indian life. However, the roar of the engines frightens the animals, who flee, and the tiger becomes a man-eater because of the absence of his usual food. And since the tiger has become a killer by accident, the old man will not help the hunters, but sets fire to the brush, forcing the tiger to escape. The interlacing of so many themes results occasionally in bewildering complexity: with the flexibility and spontaneity that arises from Rossellini's remarkable gifts of observation and his ability to synthesise, small details suffice to show far-reaching repercussions. It does not much matter, then, that 35 mm footage of the peasant is intercut with 16 mm shots of the tiger. The unity of the whole derives from

Still: India – *elephants.*

the extreme coherence of the director's thought.

In the last episode, which opens with water and moves to the desert, a man is overcome by the heat of the sun. This bewilders his pet monkey, which cannot understand what has happened. The drama of the situation gains strength from the animal's unawareness. It tries to wake its master, while vultures swoop lower and lower over them. But, as in *Paisà*, we do not have time to feel pity or consternation. There is a sudden cut to a country fair where the monkey does its number, quite alone, and is thrown money, not knowing what it means or what to do with it. The monkey tries to spend the night in a temple with wild monkeys but is driven out because it still has about it the smell of man. In a single shot of remarkable beauty, the monkey's hesitant gaze directly expresses its conflict. The end is just as abrupt. The monkey, Dulip, at a fair with a new master looks up at another trained monkey performing on a trapeze. The wealth of themes evoked is as great as in the previous episode, but is combined here with an almost giddying speed in the transitions.

The film thus seems to have the form of an oddly syncopated suite with the subject stripped down to essentials. A tracking shot over cultivated land, and another over strange religious buildings, ending on a view of a mountain – that is to say, the effort of man in the presence of gods and Nature – form a simple introduction to the third section of the film. The consistency of the themes tackled and the diversity of material investigated irresistibly recall the huge synthetical task of *October*. Although *India* does not strictly use the resources of montage, at least in the traditional sense, it is conceptually even more elaborate than Eisenstein's film. With a conscious economy of means, Rossellini achieves richer and more complex associations than Bresson or Resnais. *India* repeats the stylistic principle of *Viaggio in Italia*, which can seem superficial to a spectator lacking in concentration; it takes the form like a musical movement that manages at the same time to be very fast and very slow. Very fast, because it presents, in the shortest possible time, numerous facets of life in the India of 1957–58 – sacred and profane, mystical and commonplace. Very slow, because an almost superhuman attempt at total synthesis brings out the internal harmony of a whole way of life whose progress is solemn and peaceful.

A very slow tracking shot that goes with the labourer, Nokul, on his nostalgic visit to the dam at Hirakud reveals the film's creative method. This shot both solves the problem of showing how engineering reflects man and indicates a conscious decision faithfully to show a reality in constant growth. Before setting off to work elsewhere, Nokul visits the surroundings in which he has spent the last five years of his life. He watches people working, stands entranced before the electrical installations with their strange echoes and writes his name on a stone as a souvenir. Afterwards he argues with his wife who is waiting for him in a neighbouring temple, because she is unhappy with their enforced wandering. Finally, he bathes in the artificial lake formed by the dam, at the pivotal point of the film. Such concise, but extremely accurate notations enable us to rediscover the atmosphere of *India* in 1957–58. The man meditating by the results of his labour, the contrast of old with new, the constant presence of death (recalled by the funeral pyre and the plaque commemorating the hundred and sixty-five workers who were killed during the building of the dam) and life (Nokul's work will help prevent many other people from drowning in floods), the effect of work on people's own lives, the new economic and social state of the country, the coexistence of the basic elements (earth, fire, water), and the identification of what might be termed 'actual time' and 'historic time'. The film begins with scenes of the crowd: millions of passers by. They return at the end, symbolising the enormous population of the country. The real India contains fifteen hundred different races and adds up to a sixth of the entire population of the world. From the crowd we go on to Nature, animals, work and life in an attempt to sketch out their close but complex relationship. As in *Paisà*, through a simple statement of facts, a whole country appears before us in a brief but comprehensive representation.

In its adherence to a ceaselessly changing reality (expressed in recurrent use of the lateral tracking shot), *India* reveals its most original feature. Unlike other documentaries, *India* does not attempt to reach conclusions. It lays no claim to making any definitive judgements on

Still: India – *the old man.*

the reality of a country. *India* shows a world that is constantly developing and supplies appropriate images that change the next moment. The film recognises that the only truth lies in the moment just captured, for the cinema can only recover, with authenticity, a single moment of development. *India* is the perhaps first documentary in the history of the cinema not to try setting up facts congealed in an unchangeable relationship, but instead to identify with a dynamic process of growth. *India* gives a clear and valid account, expressed with unique honesty, of the huge and complex development that India was undergoing in 1957–58. It was a vast country subjected to dramatic changes within the context of a rigid, patriarchal system. As a reflection on transience and eternity, *India* – unfortunately one of Rossellini's least known films – opens a path that is entirely new to modern documentary.

Il Generale della Rovere

A seedy swindler, Vittorio Emanuele Bardone, alias Grimaldi, makes a living as go-between for the occupying German army and the patriots of Genoa in the winter of 1943. Uncovered by Colonel Müller, he is confined in the San Vittore prison in Milan and has no choice but to assume the identity of an Italian general killed by the Germans. In this disguise, he is supposed to find out the identity of the Resistance chief, Fabrizio. Horrified by the brutality and repression, and at the same time caught up in his part, Bardone chooses to be shot with other patriots in reprisals after the death of a Fascist boss in Milan, rather than reveal the secret he has discovered.

Il Generale della Rovere, like *Roma, città aperta*, is taken from a true story and marks a return to the themes of the Resistance pictures: the heroic struggle of 1943 in which faults and personal differences were forgotten in the face of the common enemy. But the film also indicates a regression to the melodramatic contrivances of *Roma, città aperta*. An opportunist becomes a general, a coward dies a hero's death, oppressors show not the slightest pity, and prison is a kingdom of terror ruled over by torture and death. The action is no longer simple and almost diagrammatic, but full of complications and secondary episodes: the arrangement by which Bardone takes an oriental sapphire as payment for saving both the son of the lawyer Borghesio, and the husband of Signora Fassio; Bardone's relationships with his mistress and Olga, the prostitute who still loves him; the death of the real General della Rovere; the partisans' schemes.

Il Generale della Rovere takes place in the same sort of environment as *Roma, città aperta, Paisà* and *Germania, anno zero*, but the ruins of Genoa, which form the setting are not authentic as the ruins of Rome, Florence and Berlin were. The war had been over for fourteen years – hence the inevitability of reconstruction, and the unconvincing streets, the debris built in the studio (for the entrance of the Kommandatur) and the painted canvas that passes for Milan when the hostages are executed at the end. But the falseness of both décor and writing is not simply material. In *Roma, città aperta* and *Paisà*, fiction became documentary and was raised to the level of history – a process that was nevertheless seen to be irreversible. *Il Generale della Rovere* simulates history in an unsuccessful attempt to achieve documentary – the falseness of the principle is ontological.

And Rossellini himself had changed since 1944. By 1959, he had *India* behind him. He had proclaimed the decline of fiction and heralded the reign of documentary. Paradoxically, though, it was the failure of *India* that had led to *Il Generale della Rovere*. Rossellini was not deeply involved with the swindling, heroic general. 'I have made only two purely alimentary films when I needed money to put me ahead, *Il Generale della Rovere* and *Anima Nera*. I bitterly regret them,' he stated when presenting *La Prise de pouvoir par Louis XIV* at Venice in 1966.

Bardone is nonetheless specifically a Rossellini hero, attaining his truth without choosing to. The film is taken from a novel by Indro Montanelli about a man who is forced to wear a uniform and is completely changed by it. The novel is also, in a way, an implicit justification of military honour. Its significance is perceptibly altered in the film by presenting a man who is not at all heroic. Instead, he has the mentality of a small-scale profiteer – immediately claiming the advantages due to his rank, stealing sugar and so on. He is also a coward

Still: Il Generale della Rovere – *the capture of the real General.*

and is frequently gripped by panic during his stay in San Vittore. Paradoxically, he acquires a little dignity only at the times when he seems most ridiculous: when he is beaten up after getting caught passing a message to the printer, Banchelli (Bardone's lack of skill will cost the accomplice his life under torture), or when he is being read a letter from the general's wife as he lies in the prison infirmary, bandaged about the head and looking like a sickly seal. In the film,

Bardone finds out the truth – the truth for him, that is – in a lie. The exact motivation of his final sacrifice, when he has already succeeded in finding Fabrizio's identity, is not explained. He is, perhaps, driven by remorse or belated feelings of patriotism or alternatively by the need to carry on with the part as a supremely histrionic gesture, like his speech to the prisoners during the bombing of San Vittore. The film's chief success lies in avoiding over-factual explanations. In reality, when it came to the point, Bardone could have acted as he did for any one of these reasons. Like *Germania, anno zero* and *Europa '51, Il Generale della Rovere* is unconventional in its refusal to pass judgement and in its open contradiction of our rudimentary ideas on psychology.

The feeling of period, although inevitably false, helps to make the main character convincing. There is an almost complete identification between character and actor. It is not known what Vittorio Emanuele Bardone was really like, but here he is amazingly like Vittorio De Sica. He has the same gentlemanly ways and greying hair. Women are attracted to him and he is to some extent an older version of the *jeune premier* of *Rose Scarlatte* or *Maddelena, zero in condotta*. He is equally something of a ham, after an audience at any price – taking his place among the hostages, he scrawls a few words of farewell on the photo sent by della Rovere's wife, while Müller looks on, dumbfounded. He has also the same frequently disarming sincerity. This identification is sometimes augmented with rather perverse private jokes, such as the cry '*Vittoria per Vittorio!*' when Bardone, on the telephone, announces the forthcoming release of Borghesio's son. In this respect *Il Generale della Rovere* emerges surprisingly as an examination of Rossellini's ideas on directing actors.

The development of the principal character is not expressed through specific events of life in San Vittore, but by subjective impressions – the maze of voices, noises, messages and graffiti that surrounds Bardone as soon as he arrives in the prison – and by small anecdotes which are diluted in force by their own accumulation. This is the weakness of *Il Generale della Rovere* in relation to the director's earlier work. The impartial observation of a character through his most trivial acts is still there as intention, as we see in the excellent scene when Bardone goes home in the early morning. But the lack of conviction becomes obvious, for instance, in his meeting with Fabrizio after a night of interminable waiting. Certainly Rossellini's method is still identifiable but it is in an impure version, watered down for popular consumption. Although there are very understandable reasons of politics and prestige for the huge success of this stylistic digest, it is startling proof of the misinterpretation of Rossellini's work at the time. His ideas had been labelled once and for all as being relevant only in the field of reportage and in films about the Resistance.

The lack of persuasiveness is a result of the director's complete impartiality. He cannot cheat when the material does not attract him at all – a characteristic which is strikingly clear in his other pot-boiler, *Anima Nera*. But he is also beginning to be obsessed by the need to consider history in terms of the present day in the hope of achieving an analysis of contemporary human relationships – the key theme of his subsequent work. In the same spirit, he will be led with the help of his new piece of apparatus, the Pancinor or *travelling optique* (used here for the first time) to reconsider his whole idea of direction and to come up eventually with a new conception of cinematic space.

Stills: Il Generale della Rovere.

Era notte a Roma

The English Major Pemberton, Bradley, an American pilot, and Fiodor, a Russian sergeant have escaped from a concentration camp. During the final months of the occupation of Rome, they are hidden in a loft by Esperia, a young girl who earns her living on the black market. They are tracked down by Tarcisio, an unfrocked priest who works as a spy for the Germans. As they flee, Fiodor is killed. Esperia and her fiancé, Renato, a militant communist, are arrested. Pemberton and Bradley take shelter in the Antoniani palace, and then in the convent of San Salvatore in Lauro. Bradley tries to get back to the Americans who have landed at Anzio, while Pemberton hurries to help Esperia whom the Antonianis have managed to get free. Surprised by Tarcisio, Pemberton strangles him. After a long night of waiting, the Allies reach Rome.

In a church at Tor de Nona, the lame Tarcisio spies on a woman who is pretending to confess to a young priest (in fact a soldier in disguise) in order to pass him information. Esperia spots what Tarcisio is up to and points him out to Pemberton, who in turn watches him. This action, does not take long, but is complicated as it centres on the coming and going of several characters. It is presented with analytical clarity, from a single set-up by a camera endowed with quite unusual powers of movement.

This treatment is particularly insistent in the sequence of Tarcisio's death. The lame man's threats to Esperia, her reaction in tipping a pan of boiling water over him, the sudden appearance of Pemberton out of his hiding place, the fight, the strangling of Tarcisio and the Englishman's horror are all shown in one take from a single, implacable viewpoint. But this is capable at the same time of moving with the characters to concentrate on their looks, gestures and relationships. In the play on time, as well as space, real time and film time fuse and the sense of reality becomes greater – we are present at an event which seems really to be happening in front of us. This does not preclude the use of editing, which no longer happens afterwards, in the cutting room, but at the time of shooting. You could say that the movement of characters replaces the division into shots and, with help from the camera, instantly provides the most suitable angle at any moment for shooting whatever is happening. This ubiquitousness of the camera, which allows it to take up most appropriate positions within a single take, is achieved with a version of a zoom lens, the Pancinor, developed by Rossellini himself. 'The Pancinor is like a camera suspended in space: it is like having the camera in your hand. The director can put the accents where he wishes, during the shooting of the scene. Moreover, this device removes any of the rigidity attached to cutting and speeds up the rhythm because changes in angle also bring their own tempo. The dolly is used specifically for changes of angle, while moving in or out is done with the Pancinor. Cutting, then, restricts the acting: the actor has to keep stopping and taking up a new position. Instead, the director can thus steal the expressions of the actors without their noticing him, while their performance goes on.' This was how the director explained his method in the book containing the script of *Era notte a Roma*. His statement is most important since it implies a whole new idea of *mise-en-scène* and space in the cinema. In particular, it reveals the main significance of *Era notte a Roma*. Unlike *Roma, città aperta* and *Paisà*, which otherwise it closely resembles, it is no longer concerned only to show but also to analyse.

This intention materialises through a constant effort to draw back and give the camera a better perspective on the action. The Pancinor gives a remarkable emphasis to the end of the first scene, when the car carrying the fake nuns makes off into a wide open landscape, as if to underline the transition between the external world and the claustrophobic interiors which is an essential of the film. The same also goes for the scene in which Don Valerio reads the account of the Fosse Ardeatine massacre, and the camera draws back from a close up of his face to show everyone in the refectory of San Salvatore at Lauro. This movement so emphasises the systematic integration of characters in a group that it brings out the choral nature of the film. This is not purely a physical movement back by the camera; it is also conceptual. At the beginning, Major Pemberton talks off-screen for the only time in the film and recalls his own memory of the help given by Italians to Allied soldiers escaping from German camps. They were inspired not only by interest or conviction but also often by a spirit of Christian charity. This commentary, though never repeated, is enough (*Era notte a Roma* is not placed in the area of subjectivity) to give a retrospective aspect to the story, which is taken from an already distant past and is thus a subject for reflection.

After the mention of Christian charity, we see three women disguised as nuns working for the black market. They are forced to harbour three escaped prisoners, whom they later try unsuccessfully to ditch. It is important to note that *Era notte a Roma* also operates from the distance peculiar to irony. It offers an ironical picture of reactions which, apart from being funny, provide a starting point in understanding the characters. Example a) Language: Esperia, who is getting out of her nun's clothes, is interrupted by Pemberton looking for tea. He says '*Io voglio* tea' but she interprets 'tea' as '*te*' and picks up a knife to defend herself from such libidinous intentions. Example b) Ideologies: the nuns, although they are frauds,

cross themselves when they learn that Fiodor, the third prisoner, is Russian and the chauffeur – perhaps the image of the conventional Italian – is also scandalised. Renato, however, as a militant young communist, kisses him joyfully, crying 'Tovarich!' Example c) Culture: when Colonel von Kleist arrives unexpectedly in the Antoniani household, Pemberton pretends to be the major-domo. But when the German attributes to Shelley the lines from Childe Harold quoted by the Prince, '*Quando cadrà il Colosseo, cadrà Roma, e quando cadrà Roma, cadrà il mondo*', he cannot avoid letting slip the correction, 'Byron!' In its use of humour, *Era notte a Roma* puts forward quite a complex statement of historical facts plus an analysis of the national types and idiosyncrasies thrown together by war, whereas the main concern of *Roma, città aperta* and *Paisà* was to take from life a reality which was still painfully recent, without paying too much attention to the nuances.

This intention of *Era notte a Roma* is made clear simply in the choice of the main characters – an English major, an American lieutenant and a Russian sergeant, whose exemplary, even didactic nature is beyond question. The others all correspond in some way to the characters of *Roma, città aperta*. Esperia is the counterpart of Pina, Renato that of Manfredi and Don Valerio that of Don Pietro. As in *Roma, città aperta*, each is identified with the image of the whole city, particularly Esperia, whose tears at the end echo Pina's tears of long before. They are brought together by the same feeling of community – the constantly retreating camera (as in the scene at San Salvatore) always moves towards ensembles – and by the same struggle for freedom. They, too, are all protagonists but are shown to us from a different angle: they are portrayed less through their actions than through their relationships with foreigners, by the idea of the world that an Englishman, an

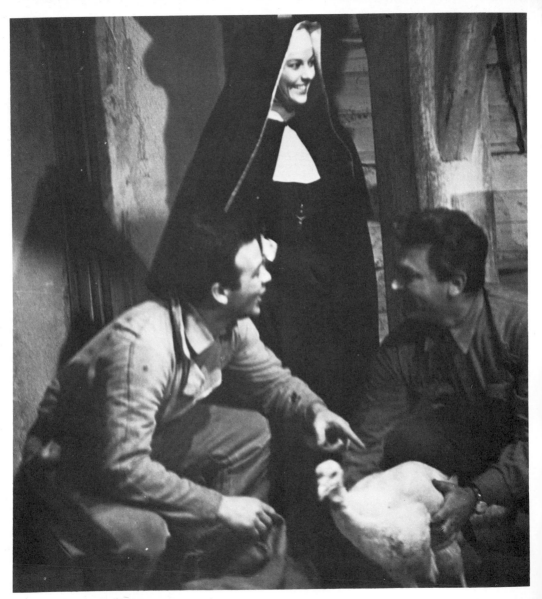

American or a Russian can bring them. The scene which most embodies the film's premise in this respect is the Christmas in the attic. Fiodor struggles for the words to thank his friends in Italian. Ashamed that he cannot express his feelings as he would like, the sergeant goes on in his own language, with a long, impassioned and moving soliloquy. The foreign words in no way prevent the others from grasping his meaning. The description of Italian behaviour goes much further than this: to understand how much more comprehensive and subtle this picture of Roman society is than the sketch in *Roma, città aperta*, you have only to consider the short but revealing appearance of Prince Antoniani. He is also a symbol of Rome, and a man with all the traditional cunning of a servant of the Vatican and the education and polish required to affect a courteous tolerance of the enemy in his home.

Like that of *Il Generale della Rovere*, the décor is, at least partially, reconstructed, but it has a different atmosphere. The décor of the previous film had a simple scenic function and was reduced to the face of the star (whose emotions formed the centre of interest) and the prison (the psychological image of the prison the whole country had become for Italians). In *Era notte a Roma*, the setting is constricted to the extent that we are seeing it from the point of view of three prisoners, but real. From their window, they can see only the roofs of Rome, which had not undergone any essential change since 1945. The working-class district of Tor de Nona, where Esperia's house and most of the action are situated, has also changed little. The impression of falseness given by *Il Generale della Rovere* is avoided here.

The activity of the phoney nuns in the country during the exodus of the refugees with

Still: Era notte a Roma – *Bradley, Esperia, Fiodor and the turkey.*

their poor possessions – the opening sequence – provides a faithful image of the insecurity outside. From there we go to the interior world where the characters find shelter – the loft of Esperia's house, the Antoniani residence, the convent of San Salvatore in Lauro. These sets shape the whole film, particularly the enclosed, almost motherly space of the loft, which is also a way into the world of dreams and fantasy. As he enters, Fiodor lights up a room where a statue of a horse rises surprisingly out of the ground. In the next room, Pemberton dislodges the candle from an angel's outstretched hand. The décor is none the less realistic for all this sophistication. The attic belongs to Prince Antoniani, Esperia's protector. Even the workshop, decorated with antique statuary, where members of the Resistance make bombs, remains a place of repose and protection. For the characters to come out of this setting means certain danger. Fiodor's expedition into the street to retrieve an escaped turkey seriously threatens the security of them all. It can even mean death. Fiodor is killed by the SS as he leaves the workshop, where he has been helping the Resistance; Renato is later captured and shot. The Antoniani Palace and the convent of San Salvatore – always presented in opposition to the external world – are extensions of the friendly shelter of the attic. We are quite intentionally shown, several times and in detail, that the only way back to the security of these places is across the roofs of Tor de Nona. By refusing to leave this environment – unlike Bradley who risks everything to rejoin the Allies at Anzio – Pemberton saves his own life and that of Esperia when she is threatened by Tarcisio. The visual *leit-motiv* of St Peter's dome, the universally accepted symbol of Rome, which was previously seen in the last shot of *Roma, città aperta*, is visible from the various locations – the attic, the palace, the monastery and over

the roofs. It is the first thing the escaped prisoners see on the day after their arrival in the Eternal City (Pemberton quotes Virgil), and it links the settings together under its protective outline.

The décor represents not only three different social strata – the people, the aristocrats and the clergy – but also the close bond they develop in order to survive. This arouses Tarcisio's terrible curse: '*Di Roma non resterà pietra su pietra!*' Before leaving Esperia's house in self-imposed punishment for his carelessness, Fiodor makes all his friends sit down in a circle in a clear

Still: Era notte a Roma – *in the attic; the Englishman, Pemberton, the American, Bradley, the Italian doctor and the Russian, Fiodor.*

ritual of community and safety. The fake priests foil Tarcisio's plan to unmask them by reciting the Adoration of the Cross in unison. It is only in this harmony that it is possible to escape death. But the film's choral nature is important in giving further depth of meaning. Bourgeois, aristocrats, communists, priests real and unfrocked, Resistance workers, doctors, soldiers and the occupying army – the whole conglomeration of characters embodies a comprehensive image of society and ultimately contributes to *Era notte a Roma* its full significance. The interest does not come entirely from looking at historical events as they happen. They are also reconsidered from the standpoint of today. It is no longer enough to give an account of history; it has also to be examined critically.

Era notte a Roma has a great range of characters (unlike Rossellini's later films which are practically based on one person), an abundance of peripheral dramatic incidents and some exaggerated characterisations, the main example being Tarcisio, who is an ugly, lame, unfrocked priest – though his very excess gives him an almost Dostoievsky feeling. Yet it is not a melodramatic film by virtue of an exposition that is sometimes staggeringly simple. Example: after Renato's death, Pemberton thinks about Esperia while he is walking on the terrace at San Salvatore. There is an immediate cut to the Major coming in through the attic window after crossing the roofs. Despite such narrative speed, the film lasts one hundred and forty-five minutes, which gives some idea of its complexity. Other factors, too, keep melodrama away. There is the overtly didactic concept: the relationships between Italians, English, Germans, Russians and American in *Era notte a Roma* provide an image of Europe, even the world. On the other hand, the plot, in giving a clear, uncomplicated outline of the fugitives' journey – they travel South from the Po to Rome, the opposite direction from *Paisà* – the film also symbolises a spiritual journey. On their way, Pemberton and Esperia discover other people as well as a capacity to give of themselves. The end is focused on Esperia's tears, in an atmosphere of sadness. Even if the liberation has come, it has still to be completed. The theme may be taken from the past, but the film speaks for today.

Viva l'Italia!

After the rising at Palermo on 3 April 1860 has failed, Giuseppe Garibaldi prepares an expedition to take the Two Sicilies and force Italian unity; he is helped secretly by the minister Cavour. At the head of a thousand red-shirted volunteers, Garibaldi sets out from Marsala, beats the Bourbon troops at Calatafimi and captures Palermo. Leaving Cavour now openly trying to organise a regular government on the island, Garibaldi crosses the Straits of Messina on the night of 18–19 August. On 7 September, he enters Naples which has been abandoned by the Bourbon king, Francis II. The Thousand successfully defend the town in the Battle of Volturno and prepare a march on Rome to achieve national unity. Political fluctuations and Cavour's intrigues force Garibaldi to yield to the will of the king, Victor Emmanuel, at a meeting in Teano. Garibaldi is placed in reserve and goes into voluntary exile on the island of Caprera.

Alessandro Blasetti's *1860* (1933), the first film about the Risorgimento has Giuseppe Garibaldi walking among his men, before the battle at Calatafimi, declaiming his famous speech '*Qui si fa l'Italia o si muore!*' Transformed into a mythical figure, he remains invisible, as his progress is suggested by subjective camera-movements. It is entirely faithful to a heroic tradition in the cinema and is not lacking in strength. The aim is obviously to dramatise historical fact and to add the desired emphasis to the events shown. *Viva l'Italia!* (1960) was an assignment made for the Italian government as part of the centenary celebrations of the Risorgimento. The same scene is treated quite differently. Giuseppe Garibaldi eats bread and cheese, asks for salt and then in a lengthy, static shot, explains that the slope of the land offers tactical advantages against General Landi's

army, calmly concluding '*Qui si fa l'Italia o si muore!*' as a quiet acceptance of fact. This contrasting treatment of the event is in itself enough to indicate the tone of *Viva l'Italia!*

The film opens with a concise explanation of the historical and political background on the soundtrack, while the camera moves away from the Italian peninsula on the map to pick out Sicily. Whenever necessary, for example during the advance of the Thousand towards Palermo, maps are used to make the explanations clearer and more concise. Exposition takes precedence here over aesthetics. The most important

Stills: Viva l'Italia! – *Garibaldi moves among his troops; the attack at Calatafimi.*

battles of Garibaldi's campaign – Calatafimi, Messina and Volturno – are given a documentary, informative treatment without attempts to add drama or spectacle. Logical explanations are given of the tactical aims to be achieved, and the movement of forces in the field are shown with topographical precision. At Calatafimi, Garibaldi's men have to climb a slope to reach the high ground where General Landi overlooks the battlefield. Far from being a disadvantage,

this favours the attackers by preventing Landi from using his cannon. The ability of the Pancinor to cover enormous stretches of the landscape allows sweeping movements which can simultaneously show both fighting forces, thus giving a comprehensive picture of the battle. At Messina, a single, very long and mobile take, panning round through a full circle, takes in the site of Garibaldi's camp, scans the Calabrian coast and the Straits, continues past the Milazzo lighthouse on the peak overlooking the Sound, and returns to the Thousand's headquarters. These scenes do not add up to allegorical criticisms of war, like those in Vittorio Cottafavi's *I Cento Cavalieri* (1964) or Orson Welles's *Chimes at Midnight* (1965), nor are they heroic tableaux. The battles have neither horror nor beauty, but are just battles, historical occurrences objectively examined with the detachment of a diarist. The Pancinor is very important here, since its extreme ease of movement allows the direct presentation of action from a wide variety of angles. The characteristic flattening out of perspectives gives the appearance of a moving fresco, the ideal medium for a historical subject. The zoom

is at last recognised as having more than purely technical value. Rossellini's zooms are always very slow, and he makes the optical effect imperceptible by combining it with the movement of characters in the scene. Its use intensifies the impression of urgency – the feeling that we are watching a reportage of events in the present – the most faithful restoration of the past.

Francis II's flight from his court at Naples

Stills: Viva l'Italia!

and Garibaldi's meeting with Victor Emmanuel at Teano show the same intention of presenting events as they happen, without bias. Their dramatic weight in the film depends entirely on the context and their historical significance. The picture of Garibaldi is very human: he is rheumaticky, coughs and has to put on his spectacles to read out the campaign objectives of the Thousand, or the decree of Italian unity. He hums during the evaluation of the military possibilities at Calatafimi. In every situation he remains completely calm: he waits until noon before giving the order to join battle and provide '*due bastonate a questi signori*'; he pays no attention to the loss of his standard in this encounter; at Volturno, he decides on defensive tactics. At all times he is available to everyone: visiting enemy soldiers wounded in the first battle and congratulating them on their courage, '*Bravi ragazzi, avete lottato bene*'; eating with country people after his meeting with the king at Teano. All this, then, shows the intention of turning a historical figure and almost a myth in Italy, into a character, pure and simple. This extraordinarily human portrayal is the first given by Rossellini of an *active* hero, who makes things happen rather than just submitting to them as in the previous films.

With only two digressions, Rosa's sacrifice and the exile of Francis II, *Viva l'Italia!* takes the form of a simple chronicle of the campaign carried out by the Thousand as described in existing historical sources, Bandi's journal, the memoirs of Abba, Dumas père, etc. Despite being an official celebratory assignment, the film presents Garibaldi as just another character in the progress of history, placed within his phenomenological background – certainly not as a legendary hero. Moreover, all the facts given can be found in history books and scrupulous care is taken to be objective and accurate. Admittedly, however, the people (like Cavour and La Farina) and the political questions (such as the monarchy) needed for a *full* understanding of the episode's subtler points remain peripheral to the film. The attempt to portray the spirit and meaning of a whole historical period through a clear-cut event like the campaign of the Thousand, is such a complex task that, inevitably, the director has had to concentrate on the most accessible facts and select the most important.

After Calatafimi, Garibaldi's men, who have fought through to success side by side with monks and peasants, crowd round to acclaim their leader and one of them calls out '*Hai visto, Giuseppe Garibaldi, quello che siamo stati capaci di fare?*' The men who managed this were just the 'few ill-armed bourgeois with two old cannon, led by a man called Garubardo,' as they were described in the first report that General Landi received of the Thousand setting out from Marsala. The intention of *Viva l'Italia!* was to give prominence to the en-thusiastic, even naïve, faith of a small nucleus of people in the idea of freedom for everyone, as expressed by the Redshirts. It is represented by Bandi's quiet bearing, Bixio's almost boyish forcefulness, and equally by the spontaneous impulse of Rosa, who is killed as a result of her decision to help Garibaldi's side.

The film is made up of continual forward tracking shots (a visual expression of territory covered and possessed), which are sharply inter-rupted. This is an attempt to state the opposi-tion between the sweeping movement of brother-hood, inspired by the faith of Garibaldi and his supporters, and the inert, passive Italy that is personified with invisible but threatening force in Mazzini's visit to Naples and, even more, in the meeting with Victor Emmanuel at Teano – witness the King's terse, indifferent greeting – which sadly concludes the Thousand's exploits. *Viva l'Italia!* is also the story of failure (fore-shadowed by the abortive revolt in Palermo at the beginning), of a movement not carried through, an uncompleted march to Rome and an ideal of unity unachieved: Venice remains in the hands of the Austrians and the Pontifical State survives, despite the proclamation of Victor Emmanuel as king after the election of the first Italian parliament in 1861. On the way to Palermo, Garibaldi's followers rest at the ruined temple at Segesta and are surprised that such beauty could be reduced to such wretchedness. This sudden awareness of time is an early indication of the relative, transient quality that is to characterise the Thousand's campaign and, indeed, goes with all human endeavour. When Garibaldi's troops disperse on the entry into Naples, a flock of sheep takes over the screen, recalling the sheep already encountered by the Thousand on the way to Calatafimi. This sign of nature and everyday life concludes the first cycle of Garibaldi's enterprise. Nature and life are taking their due. Now the film is not just only a chronicle; it is also an analysis, also, providing explanation as well as description.

The unexpected arrival of a French journalist at Palermo; the meeting with Alexandre Dumas, whom Garibaldi refers to as 'the great poet'; the military band seen resting in the wood before getting into line and sweating as they play the Thousand into Calabria; the mayor who presents Garibaldi with the key to his village while the local poet declaims his praise of 'Garubardo': these touches all good-naturedly recall the atmosphere of the period with extraordinary accuracy. Garibaldi's encounter with the Bourbon generals who have come to negotiate an honourable peace is also notable for its spontaneity: Garibaldi is eating an orange and offers a piece to the visitors. This

Still: Viva l'Italia!

detail is quite consistent with Rossellini's style, but the director has filmed it just as it appears in Bandi's diary. This attitude enables him to translate the past miraculously into the present throughout the entire film. Nothing seems predetermined and everything is revealed with an overriding simplicity. When the Thousand reach the square at Palermo, an extremely long tracking shot follows Garibaldi up and down the steps, past ancient statues. The perfect integration of man, history and film is sufficient proof of the artistic synthesis that has gone into *Viva l'Italia!* The combination of ethics and

Vanina Vanini

Still: Viva l'Italia! – *Garibaldi (Renzo Ricci) and Bandi (Franco Interlenghi).*

In 1824, Pietro Missirilli, a member of the rain to a secret meeting of the *carbonari* at Via one of his companions from Romagna. He is wounded while trying to escape the police and finds shelter with Prince Asdrubale Vanini, who is very well acquainted with the Roman court and is a lover of Countess Vittoleschi. The aristocrat's youngest daughter, Vanina, finds Pietro's hiding place and falls in love with him, becoming his mistress. When he becomes a leader of the carbonari, Pietro leaves Vanina, although she wants to keep him with her in her castle at San Nicolò. She therefore denounces the conspirators to the Vatican police. Pietro shamè-facedly gives himself up. Vanina obtains his pardon from Cardinal Savelli, but Pietro furiously spurns her on finding out the truth. At the moment of his execution, Vanina goes into a convent.

aesthetics is the basis of Rossellini's unusual ability to place himself in the time of the events he is describing. *Viva l'Italia!* fulfils the aspiration towards history 'lived as the present' first shown *Francesco, giullare di Dio*, which is to hagiography what *Viva l'Italia!* is to history. *Viva l'Italia!* also makes explicit the meaning behind the experiment begun in *Era notte a Roma*, which is similarly conceived in the form of a factual chronicle, however much this may be obscured by its fictional character and by its forced dependence on an iconography already much exploited in the cinema (even by Rossellini himself, though with a different purpose). These other motifs confuse the issue, but in *Viva l'Italia!* there is no longer any doubt, and the measure of its success is immediately striking.

The young Pietro makes his way through the rain to a secret meeting of the *carbonari* at Via Margutta. He takes part, fascinated, in a ceremony that tires the elderly leader of the conspirators, and joins in a lively discussion which is interrupted by the police. They have been alerted by the traitor Pontini, already suspect for his weakness and dandyism. This sequence might have come from almost any period film, and there have been plenty to choose from. But the abundance of accuracy of detail concerning the ceremonial of the meeting – girl dressed in man's clothes and smoking a pipe, the characters' gestures – recalls the heavily staged rituals of the Freemasons, as well as of the *carbonari*. It even extends the image of the kind of revolutionary folklore we saw in the juvenile forcefulness of Nino Bixio's cries to his country and his polished bow as he kisses the hand of the French journalist in *Viva l'Italia!* Equally, this scene explains the elated and romantic attitude of the cultured middle classes in Italy during the first half of the nineteenth century, roused as they were against church and aristocracy by the example of the French revolution. From the outset, then, Pietro seems imprisoned by a setting. Intent on action, he can only play out a destiny history has decided.

When Princess Vanina Vanini arrives at the ball, a eunuch is discussing Roman women with a German. Their conversation – which is taken from another Stendhal work, 'De l'amour' – fixes Vanina in her social and historical context, as well as enabling the audience to keep its distance from these characters, simply because they are at once judges and members of the world in question. There is obvious complicity between Prince Vanini and Cardinal Savelli, whom everyone picks out as the next Pope and who is already considering the expediency of banning the waltz at court. The power held by Church and aristocracy over Italian society in 1824, after the end of the French hegemony, denotes the triumph of reactionary forces in the country. At the same time, the waltz is a symbol of a society in which Vanina, although she is part of it, seems ill at ease. Like Pietro, the princess is a prisoner of her environment and of a particular historical situation; her meeting with Pietro already seems inevitable. At the end of the ball, news comes of an escaped *carbonaro* who has eluded the police. The ball scene also establishes the whole structure of the film in which, as in the Stendhal story (in 'Chroniques Italiennes') from which *Vanina Vanini* is taken, narration, description and even analysis are inseparable at every level.

A fine example of the synthetical structure in which events are presented is the scene in which the herald announces new restrictions, threatening death to anyone who helps the *carbonari*, while a wide circular panning movement with the Pancinor shows faces set in silent anger. As in *Viva l'Italia!*, the use of the zoom is intended to show multiple aspects of a situation and to restore it in the form of a moving fresco, while imparting to it the urgency of reportage, the feeling of history being filmed as it happens. The citizens' revolt that follows the proclamation has a similar feeling of urgency.

'When the soldiers rush up to the dead man in the crowd, they examine the hands of the people standing nearby. Each man has blood on his hands, thereby asserting the collective responsibility of the kind referred to in the proclamation. We dissolve into a picture of green countryside. We see a man running. We hear a gun shot. The man falls to the ground in direct line with a cascading waterfall in the distance. The community of man and nature is carried over into the next image of a forest clearing. A man on horse-back rides up and calls out. Other men come out from behind the trees to listen to what he is saying. We hear nothing of what he says and we don't need to because the image does all the work. Some trees are standing, many have already been felled and are strewn about chaotically. To the left there is a neat pile of cut logs. There is a small fire burning in the centre of the image. This picture summarises the state of Italy in general and the rebellion in particular: both have been arrested in their development, in their growth. The old has not been cut down and the new has not been put to use. As in the previous shot man was linked to the landscape; in this shot the rebellion is linked to Italy.

'The fire symbol in the forest is taken up during the next sequence, at the fair, in which we see a fire-eater blowing flames from his mouth. The fire of the rebellion has become ineffectual: prisoners are being led, chained to one another, across the square; two men are placed in the stocks; a whipping has just been ordered.'

This series of actions, so well analysed by Paul Mayersberg in Movie 6 remarkably sums up the failure of revolutionary efforts in Italy at this point. They were to fail again in 1830 and 1848, until the declaration of national unity in 1860 (to which the background was recorded in *Viva l'Italia!*). The visual structure (sets, costume, colours and so on) is as important as the dramatic construction in recreating the characters' social, historical and psychological environment. At the investiture of a cardinal, the princes of the Church are dressed in red, while members of the court wear black. This is

Stills: Vanina Vanini – *Pietro among the carbonari and with Vanina in the castle.*

contrary to convention but historically correct. We see the same distribution of colours in Vanina's visit to Cardinal Savelli, but here, history is less important than the irony of the future Pope's obvious sexual desire for the princess. The *black* soutane of the young confessor, whose impassioned words leave such a burning impression on Vanina, is also ironical in this respect. At the end, Pietro is put to death on a scaffold that is significantly painted red, flanked by soldiers clad in black. This leaves no possible doubt as to the meaning of his revolt and his death, while also remaining faithful to Stendhal's own particular mythology of colour, since 'Vanina Vanini' and '*Le Rouge et le noir*' were written in the same period and have obvious affinities.

The carefully realistic account of the external world satisfies more than the demands of pure reportage. It makes clear the effect this world has on the love of Pietro and Vanina, which is never looked at in an introspective way. Even when they are hidden away in the peace and shelter of the castle at San Nicolò, the things that keep them apart are always clear. Vanina may seem perfectly at ease in a dress that goes with the décor, but Pietro's buckskin waistcoat makes clear his social inferiority and his connection with the world outside. The many love scenes often turn into discussions of social and political questions in what could be an ironic variation on the well-worn story of an aristocrat's affair with a poor student. More simply, the theme follows Stendhal's statement in the original that 'one of General Bonaparte's words echoed bitterly in the heart of this young

man and influenced his entire behaviour in respect of women.' The original text is followed absolutely, in feeling as well as construction. Where one sentence is enough for Stendhal to explain Vanina becoming Pietro's mistress, 'soon she had nothing left to refuse him', Rossellini makes óne shot tell us the same thing.

Stills: Vanina Vanini – *Vanina and Pietro* (*below*); *Vanina visits Cardinal Savelli* (*opposite*).

However, this faithful interpretation is logical, considering how anxious Stendhal is to tell us in the novel that in 1796, when the statesmen of Brescia told General Bonaparte that the Brescians loved liberty more than any other Italians, he commented, 'Yes, they like to talk about it to their mistresses.' Like Stendhal, Rossellini has shown a clear tendency throughout his work to describe important events through individual behaviour.

Vanina Vanini does not set out only to record a love story but to disclose the precise social and political factors that dominate the characters, whose destiny is connected with that of Italy – the director at first wanted to call it *Chronique Italienne*. Pietro's affair with Vanina provides him with the sexual freedom he needs as a possible means to attaining the social freedom he wants. But this sexual freedom becomes an impediment to political liberty: while he is hiding in the castle at San Nicolò, he finds that he is more of a slave than ever. At the end, when Vanina tells him that she has obtained his pardon from Cardinal Savelli and confesses to the betrayal, he hits her with his chains in front of a religious triptych depicting the Virgin Mary. It is finally in taking on captivity upon himself that he confirms his freedom; his choice enables him to die a free man. The last shot shows Vanina running distractedly and ringing at the convent door. She will, perhaps, like Irene Girard in *Europa '51*, find her liberty paradoxically in prison, after her abortive attempts throughout to free herself in confession. A moment before going in, she looks round and meets the glance of Pietro who has made an identical movement as he climbs the scaffold. The film seems to have no aim but to catch this brief moment in eternity. When the convent door is closed, the camera tracking along behind Vanina stops short. Her future remains as open as that of Karin in *Stromboli, terra di Dio*, though in the novel the girl hypocritically opts for marriage with Cardinal Savelli's nephew. Rossellini's films end simply when their characters achieve a certain state of consciousness.

It is now possible to understand that *Vanina Vanini* is the logical extension of the experiment begun in *Era notte a Roma* and developed in *Viva l'Italia!*, helping complete the consideration of the Risorgimento embarked on by the latter. A balance is also sought between individual and collective, between the moment lived and the concept of history. In this respect it is useful to compare *Vanina Vanini* with Luchino Visconti's *Senso* (1954) which is also a romantic melodrama and superficially resembles it. Each film deals with an affair that destroys those concerned, Countess Serpieri and Lieutenant Mahler, Princess Vanini and Pietro Missirilli. But *Senso* would clearly like to bring history into line with the recent past

and associates the revolutionary patriots of the Risorgimento with the partisans of the 1940's and the political militants of the 1950's, in the same way as *Fellini Satyricon* claims a connection between ancient Romans and hippies. *Senso*, then, is concerned with discussion presented as history on the pattern of a Georg Lukács reinterpretation of a nineteenth-century novel – an attempt is made to force on the audience meaningful fiction with tendentious aims. The role of Count Ussoni, symbol of an ideal future, particularly fits this scheme. *Vanina Vanini*, however, lays no claim to comparing ancient history with modern, though this was clearly the intention in the · first treatment written by Franco Solinas and Antonello Trombadori but, according to Mario Verdone, rejected by Rossellini, causing a bitter row. There is no wish to provide a judgement in advance, but only to rediscover a historical past as spontaneously and accurately as possible, in all its complexity, leaving the events to speak for themselves. Rossellini has fused together a variety of work by Stendhal – fiction ('Vanina Vanini'), essay ('De l'amour'), and journal ('Les Promenades dans Rome', 'Naples Rome Florence') – in his attempt to produce a work of historical research which is presented for our consideration in a documentary manner.

The film met with general lack of understanding from the critics as well as the producer – it went through several stages of editing which distorted its meaning in the copies that were distributed; only one complete, or almost complete, copy has been preserved and is in the Cinémathèque Française. The film was never seen in the right perspective – as the highly stimulating continuation of Rossellini's treatise on historical films and realism in the cinema. Its importance was not to be recognised until the dazzling success of *La Prise de pouvoir par Louis XIV*.

Anima Nera

Adriano marries Marcella after inheriting property from a friend in Turin, who has died in an accident; they settle in Rome. While he is occupied with business, his young wife learns from Alessandra, the dead friend's sister, that her husband's relationship with him was a doubtful one. She panics and leaves home. Although Adriano is very much in love with Marcella, he seeks relief in the arms of an old friend, Mimosa, a prostitute. When Marcella returns, it is Mimosa who shows them the faults each has committed. Adriano will be able to embark on a more worthy life, with his wife's help, only if he renounces his doubtful heritage.

The credits appear on a background of anonymous faces, with crowd noises on the soundtrack. A subjective tracking shot later shows the outskirts of Pisa and its monuments. In this tourist centre the young couple spend their wedding night. As in *Viaggio in Italia*, we start from the outside world, Italy, and penetrate the privacy of a couple. At the end, the crowd noises return over a visual of Adriano's shamed face. The conclusion is ironic as the initial

scenes are followed by a very different image of Italy and its people. The wife is a bigot with all the bourgeois catholic prejudices and leaves her husband after their first serious quarrel. The husband is a weak, small-time shyster who has tried to make his fortune after a rather less than glittering past, notable for homosexual escapades.

Stills: Anima Nera.

When his wife leaves him, Adriano seems strangely alienated from his surroundings. He lies down on the bed, smokes, puts on a record, twice telephones his friend Mimosa to arrange a date and sniffs Marcella's perfume on the pillow. This lost-child impression – accentuated by the camera following relentlessly in a long, continuous take – becomes almost unbearable at the end. After the painful confrontation with his wife, Adriano leans out of the window

towards an uncertain future, the very image of shame. He is a victim of his past – a homosexual incident with a German officer during the occupation taught him to turn his charms to advantage in the minor upheavals that followed the war, the reward being the property of the young aristocrat from Turin. Adriano is as much the product of a particular historical situation as little Edmund, captivated by a spurious morality in *Germania, anno zero*. But there the context shapes the very structure of the film, while *Anima Nera* contains only a reference to it and the plot never rises above the most superficial melodrama.

Marcella is clearly a victim of her own middle-class prejudices rather than of the unpleasant things Alessandra has to say. The sister of the missing aristocrat lies in wait for her, moving in circles, like a spider around her prey (a situation similar to that of Irene and Joanna in *La Paura*). Having left, almost fled, her family to marry Adriano, she lets her whole happiness collapse at the first serious threat. It is a prostitute who explains to her the unpleasant facts about her behaviour. The blow she receives is that much harder because she really loved Adriano very much. This is revealed especially in the two long scenes of waking up after the wedding night and of their arrival at the apartment which has no furniture except a bed. The splendid acting and the freedom of the characters, closely watched with the Pancinor, give the scene a direct, intense sensuality rarely seen in the cinema – particularly in Rossellini's films which are very sensual, but devoid of erotic sequences. The scenes are reminiscent of the sexual quality of parts of Joseph Losey's *Blind Date* (1959). *Anima Nera* is at its most worthwhile when it concentrates on following and recording the characters' reactions, unencumbered by the conventions of the plot.

Visible opposition to the love of Marcella and Adriano comes in the shape of Alessandra and Olga, the young man's business associate. The two women are, oddly enough, typed as 'thirties vamps, straight out of the *fumetti*. The character of Mimosa is meant to be more than the usual whore-with-a-heart-of-gold, but her part in the plot is enough to ensure that she conforms to such an outmoded stereotype. *Anima Nera* might be considered the same sort of return to melodrama that *Il Generale della Rovere* was to the cinema of the Resistance. In that case it falls between the pure tragedy of *Una Voce Umana* and the examination in *La Paura* of a dramatic event in the light of an actual historical situation. Since it cannot compare with either alternative, *Anima Nera* is stuck at the level of a weepie.

There are some good moments of authenticity caught with the Pancinor, but in some agonisingly long-held shots, the camera angles are as well worn as the dramatic construction. It is real torture to see the director of *Paisà* and *Viaggio in Italia* resorting to supposedly modern movie components right down to strip-tease and sports cars. After the extreme economy and the almost miraculous spontaneity of his previous work, this is just a film. For the first time in his career, Rossellini is visibly working at Cinema.

Anima Nera is a pot-boiler in the same way as *Il Generale della Rovere*, but betrays a new lack of conviction. After outgrowing Claudel and Zweig and showing himself worthy of Stendhal, Rossellini now makes do with a pretty mediocre play by Giuseppe Patroni-Griffi. *Anima Nera*, then, stems from sad disillusionment, made worse by the failure of *Vanina Vanini*. The director is seriously reconsidering his whole work as well as the function of the cinema, the nature of contemporary art and his relationship with his audience. *Anima Nera* is a film of extraordinary sadness, because it shows Rossellini no longer believing in the cinema.

Illibatezza

In the course of a flight, Anna Maria, an air hostess on the Rome-Bangkok route, meets Joe, an American P.R. man who is studying new markets in Siam. Joe falls for Anna Maria, who tries in vain to put him off. Her fiancé, Carlo, seeks advice for her from a psychiatrist in Rome, who recommends her to change her clothes and make-up to get rid of the motherly air that is attracting Joe. Anna Maria turns into a sexy platinum blonde. Joe is a keen as Carlo to find in this new image the girl from before.

A quotation from Alfred Adler appears on the screen against a black background: 'In these days, a man often feels troubled by an indefinable *angst* and while he is at work, his unconscious urges him to find a refuge which will feed and protect him. His mother's womb. For this kind of man, even love becomes a whimpering search for the protective womb.' This imparts a sarcastic flavour to the rather ordinary story of an American public relations man who falls for an Alitalia air hostess, decides to have an affair with her and follows her through a strange setting of Buddhist priests and pagodas.

From the outset, Anna Maria seems the personification of what one might describe as an energetic, modern girl. She works as an air hostess for a major airline, travels to Siam, takes frequent showers (albeit with great modesty), is constantly on the telephone, worries about her weight and films 'everything she sees' (like Patricia Leacock in *Le Grand Escroc*, the sketch which Godard was to shoot a few months later), getting a friend to film her in turn. All this and her surroundings make

Still: Illibatezza – *Anna Maria (Rosanna Schiaffino) and Joe (Bruce Balaban).*

Anna Maria a perfect product of both consumer society and Italian puritanism. She also shows a significant desire to break the world, her world, down into images.

Joe, the American, works as a P.R. man for Rainbow beer, and is trying to increase his company's sales in Siam. He is looking for the 'Rainbow Ideal Girl'. He seems obsessed by the Playboy idea of womanhood and leafs through a copy of the magazine that contains a feature on bosoms in Hollywood. He bases his culture on the standards of television and lives by the dicta of Dale Carnegie. He, too, is a product of consumer society as well as of American puritanism. He lives entirely by appearances (and it is worth noting that in some shots he seems the exact double of Rossellini).

The presentation of Anna Maria and Joe is not intended to convey any set attitude, whether mockingly satirical or clinically observant. They are seen objectively and in their context. The method is that of *Vanina Vanini*, but with a maximum of speed and efficiency because the material is a lot less complex. In this way, we can follow their confrontation. Joe is bowled over by Anna Maria's motherly air, by her chastity – *illibatezza* – and tries to court her. She discreetly turns him down, after making

him film her in front of a pagoda, which can be taken as symbolically offering herself to him, though on a subconscious level. Deciding to stop at nothing, the American breaks in through a window of her hotel room where she has just got out of the shower – as if he were Dracula or James Bond. It is not accidental that Joe and Anna Maria behave all the time like characters they see on television. Anna Maria pushes Joe off when he tries to kiss her. He hits his head on the floor and passes out. When she tries to help him, he comes round crying like a baby. Joe's misery entirely offsets the comedy

of the situation. His suffering seems quite out of proportion to its cause.

Anna Maria's distress, shown in a quick close-up, has rapid results. In Rome, her fiancé, Carlo, has a talk with a psychiatrist friend. After examining films from Bangkok which contain several shots of Joe, the psychiatrist concludes that the man is a psychopath and a fetishist as well as suffering from an Oedipus complex. The solution is very simple: Anna Maria must change her appearance and get rid of her maternal appearance.

A new product is formed to satisfy consumer

demand. Anna Maria rather reluctantly turns into a platinum blonde and puts on sexy clothes. Joe, who is waiting for her in the hotel bar, fails to recognise her. Appearance then becomes reality, as Anna Maria starts dancing with someone and quickly becomes identified with her new image. And reality becomes appearance, when Carlo looks helplessly at the blonde Anna Maria in a film she has just sent him. Joe looks at a film of Anna Maria as a brunette and sobs like a child as he tries to kiss the motherly face which appears on his chest when he gets in the line of his projector, so that her features disintegrate into light and shadow. This excellent ending might have inspired the sequence of Michel Ange at the cinema in Godard's *Les Carabiniers*, on which Rossellini gets a screenplay credit for his adaptation of Beniamino Joppolo's play, which he directed in the summer of 1962 at the Spoleto Festival.

Illibatezza is the first sketch in *Rogopag*, which took its name from the four directors, Rossellini, Godard, Pasolini and Gregoretti, whose assignment was to describe the happy beginnings of the end of the world. It is an implacably logical essay on the dialectic of illusion and reality, a fundamental question in the cinema. It completes a didactic thesis on the idea of film realism and clarifies the significance of *Anima Nera*, which showed that the director no longer believed in the cinema, after the absolute faith of *Vanina Vanini*. *Illibatezza* was shot after Rossellini's production of 'Les Carabiniers' at Spoleto, when he had already announced his intention to cease directing films. It must be seen not only as a denunciation, but as a rejection. Joe, sobbing in front of the images he has filmed, which have ceased to belong to him, is meant to show clearly and coldly, that the cinema is only an illusion. Significantly, this is to date the last fiction film made by Rossellini and appears, on the evidence, to be his definitive farewell to the cinema.

L'Età del ferro

A documentary in five episodes, about man's development during the Iron Age, which is to say, our own period in history, from ancient times to the present day. Emphasis is given to the individual experiences of Lysis, an Etruscan, who was the first man to melt metal, and Montagnani, a metallurgist in the foundry at Piombino, who followed the removal of the Italian steel industry in German trains during World War II.

The first chapter of *L'Età del ferro* ends in a monastery, where a Chinese alchemist is experimenting with gunpowder, watched by an astonished Franciscan friar. A feeling of the period (almost that of *Francesco, giullare di Dio*) and of the clash between two different cultures is affectionately reproduced in a few moments. Immediately afterwards we see rockets successfully tested in a monastery orchard, scaring away the hens with their noise. We go from powder to guns (with one of their results the Napoleonic war, seen in shots from Abel Gance's *Austerlitz*), from bullets to vast foundries, and from primitive factories to modern rolling mills, described in all their phases of operation with the same accuracy as the shelling in *La Nave Bianca*. An attempt is made to follow the progression inherent in the facts shown, recalling at the same time their most important economic, political and social repercussions – and sometimes the most insignificant ones, like the fright of a few hens. *L'Età del ferro*, then, methodically illustrates the evolution of a mineral which has always been of importance to man.

From Lysis, the Greek merchant, to the Genoese artist and scientist, Leon Battista Alberti, from the craftsmen making armour to the small child whose urine is used to temper metal, from Mussolini and Hitler to the

metallurgist Montagnani, man is constantly present throughout the development re-created in *L'Età del ferro*. The various characters are used to assert a particular view of man, as is clearly indicated in the episode of Montagnani, which forms the whole fourth chapter. He was working in the Ilva foundry at Piombino, which was taken over by the Germans after the surrender of General Badoglio in September 1943. The fifty-six air raids on the factory during the next three months force the Germans to evacuate Piombino, taking machinery and raw materials from the Ilva works to Germany in several trains. Montagnani, thus deprived of his livelihood by the war, follows the various trains as far as Florence throughout a very hard winter, trying to identify the materials going out on each, in an all-out effort to help prevent their removal from his country. The point of this true story, which sometimes has the atmosphere of *Paisà*, is the metallurgist's instinctive compulsion to follow, not his factory, but the craft which formed his whole life and was the continuance of an ancestral

Stills: L'Età del ferro – *Lysis melts iron; the Chinese alchemist experiments with gunpowder; rockets being tried out at a monastery.*

Still: L'Età del ferro – *bombing at Piombino.*

tradition. People have been working metal in Piombino, the ancient Populonia, for three thousand years. The end of this episode justifies the unusual (and, until this point, apparently useless) length at which the work and customs of the ancient Etruscans at Populonia are dealt with in the first chapter.

Rossellini, who appears as narrator throughout the film, describes Montagnani at the start of the last chapter as one of 'those little men mixed up in the general course of history', thus making explicit a desire expressed in his previous films, to show the collective through the individual; historical changes through personal acts. In this way, the treatment of the metallurgist at Piombino is not far removed from that of other Rossellini characters – from the Sicilian girl in *Paisà*, to Nokul, the workman in *India*. He shares with the Indian the same

love for his craft, for what he has managed to do. Nokul and his thirty-five thousand companions put an end to disastrous flooding with their devotion in building the dam at Hirakud. The devotion of Montagnani, and others like him, made it possible after the war to reconstruct the Italian steel industry with materials saved from the German trains and to restore the country's economy. This is consistent with the last shot of *L'Età del ferro*, which shows huge crowds of people walking to work. We are, therefore, presented with a description and meditation on the subject of work.

This didactic purpose largely determined the structure of *L'Età del ferro*. The film draws on the most diverse sources: a) fragments of Rossellini's own films, notably *Paisà*, interestingly enough, used as newsreels; b) re-edited extracts from other films, including *Scipione l'Africano* (Carmine Gallone, 1937), *Luciano Serra pilota* (Goffredo Alessandrini, 1937) and

Austerlitz (Abel Gance, 1960); c) newsreels; d) industrial and advertising documentaries; e) the film itself, shot by Renzo Rossellini Jr, and incorporating reconstructed scenes from the more or less distant past plus others recorded in the present and the contributions of Rossellini himself as narrator. Each section of this varied material has an intrinsic value as documentation, but it gains entirely new meanings in connection with the thesis that has given rise to it. In other words, the form does not depend on a classical style of direction (composition, camera-movements, direction of actors) or on established principles of dramatic construction. Rossellini's reading of some letters from members of the Resistance, sentenced to death during the occupation, might seem pointless or misplaced from the viewpoint of traditional documentary. It does, however, create the desired atmosphere of humanity, providing an extraordinarily persuasive warmth in what he has to say. Finally, it raises the general idea of man, which echoes through the various levels of *L'Età del ferro*.

The boar-hunting sequence at the beginning of the first episode might also seem to lack an obvious justification, like the tunny-fishing in *Stromboli, terra di Dio*. But in both cases the purpose is simple: merely a question of providing realism and giving a feeling of actuality to what might merely have been reconstruction. You could equally well argue against the necessity for such scenes as the Pyrrhic dances which form part of the burial rites for the aged Rananzia (reconstructed with an awkwardness that seems entirely spontaneous, but leaving an after-taste of falseness), or the amusingly affected sixteenth-century dandy, trying on a suit of armour as if he were at the House of Dior, or the two seventeenth-century noblemen who end up by taking off their armour and fighting with their bare fists. *L'Età del ferro* loses some of its impact during its five hours'

length through boredom and repetition (for instance, of certain visual patterns in the modern industry of the last chapter) – especially if you have to sit through the whole lot at one go: it requires treatment as separate episodes on television. The characteristics of the medium were certainly considered in finally working out the handling of a subject which was intended for the widest possible transmission. *L'Età del ferro* seems less immediately concerned with forming a complete and harmonious whole, than with presenting a particular method of looking at things and launching a prototype of the cinema of the future in order to study its possible advantages and to announce the idea with an example.

In the last section, which goes from steel pressing to car production-lines, an attempt is made to analyse present-day systems of work. After the devotion of Montagnani, our respect moves from man to machine. This is remarkable in that the alienating effect of machinery on man has become one of the most renowned clichés even of the committed cinema, from *Modern Times* to *Il Deserto Rosso*. The second episode of *L'Età del ferro* concentrates on the ideas of the architect, painter, sculptor, poet and mathematician, Leone Battista Alberti, who, around 1450, was spokesman for a scientific concept of art: 'I ask of the painter that, for all his gifts, he be versed in all the liberal arts, but above all I want him to know geometry . . . Our education through which is expressed all the perfect art of painting, would be easily understood by the geometer.' It is only to be expected that Rossellini, an inventor of ingenious devices since his earliest youth and a gifted artist, should be attracted to Alberti's theories. But the film's purpose is simply to state that, from the fourteenth to the eighteenth centuries, the development of painting, sculpture and architecture was concurrent with that of mathematics, geometry, hydraulic engineering, gunnery,

Still: L'Età del ferro – *around 1400, Leon Battista Alberti was the spokesman for a scientific concept of art.*

physics, anatomy and chemistry.

Since 1961, the director has on several occasions deplored the disturbing parallel between the growing estrangement of industry and the lack of inspiration in contemporary art, which is increasingly removed from its audience, to put forward a new synthesis. The problem must have obsessed him: 'Read *Menabò* No. 4, published by Einaudi and edited by Vittorini.

There he considers whether it is possible to draw inspiration for works of art from industry, which is one of the new factors in modern life. He seems to me to conclude that this section of reality cannot act as a source of inspiration. I dare to disagree. Perhaps he wishes to say that he has not succeeded in understanding the real truth, because if one has, I am certain that things would have to happen.' This declaration was made in Rome and, several months later, he stated in Paris: 'In Italy, Vittorini has published an issue dedicated to research into the possible relationship between art and

science. The result is four hundred pages demonstrating that there is absolutely no possibility of communication. I think this shows a total lack of feeling. If a human situation exists and you look at it with feeling, it is quite impossible not to find something vital within it. It is already vital, by the simple fact of being human.' Right or wrong, this idea became a pressing subject for discussion in *L'Età del ferro*. The same thing happened before with *Europa '51*, an impassioned and urgent approach to the moral crisis that followed World War II, which can also be regarded in another sense as didactic.

Like *Europa '51*, *L'Età del ferro* is the result of deep distress, as well as the response to it: 'At a certain point I have felt . . . useless', the director admitted in 1965. The failure of his later films, made in a spirit of complete honesty and respect for his audience, and the lack of understanding which had always to some extent beset his intentions, led him to think seriously about the relationship of a work of art with the public. The failure of Dovzhenko's *Poem of the Sea* (1955-58) had also caused him anxiety: 'There is an example of a work which people did not understand. In spite of its extreme simplicity they could not make head or tail of it. That is what made me think that

everything done in the cinema is of no value from the point of view of general usefulness. There are only a few who understand. As for the majority, not only do they get nothing, but sometimes it happens that they feel offended.' This growing conviction led to Rossellini's dramatic decision to abandon the cinema altogether.

He considered for a while, restricting himself to essay-writing – with the aim 'above all of trying to see the world we live in, with new eyes, trying to find out how it is scientifically organised. Seeing it, without emotion or intuition, but with the greatest possible accuracy, as a whole.' Instead, he finally chose to make educational films. Although it is the result of a considered decision, *L'Età del ferro* seems to have the same impatient generosity as *Europa '51*. It is equally obsessed with remaining at all costs part of its time. It contains direct and indirect references, both open and implied, to almost all of Rossellini's films, from *La Nave Bianca* to *Paisà* onwards. Rossellini has been led to reconsider the whole of his earlier work, in search of another direction, another *use*. With the awkward, thrilling *L'Età del ferro*, he gives it all up and starts again, right from the beginning.

La Prise de pouvoir par Louis XIV

1661: Cardinal Mazarin is dying at his château at Vincennes. When this is confirmed by the doctors, he consults his associate, Colbert, about asking the young King, Louis XIV, to grant him an audience. His Majesty is woken up to visit the dying man and refuses the financial aid Mazarin offers him; the King cannot rely on anyone but himself. On the death of the Cardinal, he orders full mourning, his first act of authority. Louis XIV then forbids his mother, Anne of Austria, and his own brother to sit on the council and asserts his will by ordering that in future nothing will be signed or sealed without his permission. The King foils the plot of Fouquet, the steward, against his mistress, Mademoiselle de Lavalière, and has him arrested at Nantes. With Colbert, his new minister, he introduces a very strict political and economic programme. Louis XIV enlarges Versailles and, around 1682, shuts himself up there with his court, subjecting it to an extravagant and complicated code of manners. He becomes the Sun King and offers himself as a spectacle to complete his achievement of power.

At one moment in *La Prise de pouvoir par Louis XIV*, Cardinal Mazarin turns his head and dies. This extreme simplicity in showing the death of a major historical figure contrasts with the lingering death scenes that have become traditional in films of the genre. The terseness is characteristic of Rossellini's work, as in Harriet learning of her fiancé's death (*Paisà*) or Edmund's tragic decision (*Germania, anno zero*). Emotion is always condensed to obtain it at its purest. The doctors confer at the bedside, examine their patient's urine, and bleed him; Louis is awakened, and washes; Mazarin smooths colour on his cheeks before receiving the King. The opening has the impact of documentary and belongs firmly to history. Apart from functioning as pure information, the details impress us as unexpected, like the behaviour of the little monks in *Francesco, giullare di Dio*, because they are new to the cinema, escaping from the conventions built up by forty years of historical films.

After Fouquet's arrest, Colbert presents the King with his economic plan to give France industry, build up her trade, develop her agriculture and impose taxes. During his long monologue, the new minister speaks in a dull, monotonous voice, as if reading. He appears to be airing ideas that are the result of long consideration, and his quiet, thoughtful delivery forms an outstandingly accurate psychological picture. The same goes for Louis XIV's declarations, which are always colourless, in spite of the strong character they imply. Although the film is concerned with re-creating real actions, an attempt is also made to bring out the flat tone of everyday conversations between ordinary men, not actors making music with words. *La Prise de pouvoir par Louis XIV* aims at complete realism, which comes close to perfection in the art of recording reality, towards which Rossellini has been aiming since *Roma, città aperta*.

From the outset, the action is rather complicated, with the comings and goings of the doctors, Father Joly, Colbert, and Louis XIV against the disorderly background of the court. It is all seen very clearly from a single viewpoint that moves only for informational rather than dramatic reasons to follow the characters whose gestures are brought to light by the skilful combination of pans and zooms with their movements. The potentialities of the Pancinor

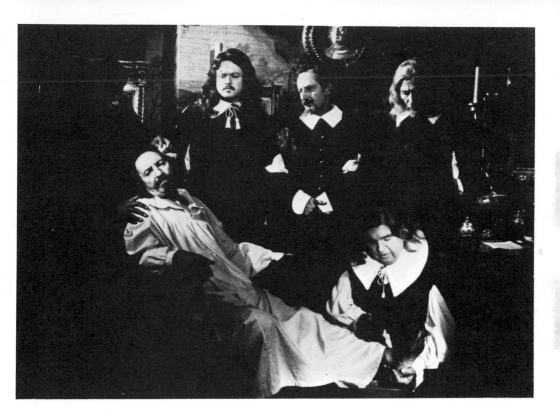

Still: La Prise de pouvoir par Louis XIV –
Mazarin is bled by his doctors.

have never been so well demonstrated. Classical
ideas of cutting and editing are questioned here
as they were in *L'età del ferro* and there is no
mise-en-scène of a traditional sort. When the
King makes a decision, he is simply filmed in
close up with the camera still, as would happen
in television reportage. Everything from the
death of Mazarin to the court formalities and
the hunt has a feeling of immediacy, of catching
events the moment they happen. The spectator

becomes like an outside witness who was there
at the time and has recorded everything he has
seen from the ideal historical viewpoint.

But the film sets its sights farther than the
mere reportage you might imagine as its limit.
The major-domo who calls for 'the King's
music' at the banquet, is preceded as he walks
by the camera tracking back. It is then that we
learn that Louis XIV is not eating alone, but in
the presence of his whole court at Versailles.
The camera moves for several reasons: a)
functional, defining the space contained in the
scene; b) dramatic, emphasising the consider-

able distance covered by the servant; c) documentary, indicating that the King's banquet is really a spectacle; d) political, showing that the whole of France – aristocrats and common people (since the advent of Hugues Capet any Frenchman has been able to see the King) – is turned towards Louis XIV. Power has been taken over and the film is coming to an end. Rossellini's method of integrating the reporting and the analysis of an event, first tried in a historical film with *Era notte a Roma*, reaches its most convincing success in *La Prise de pouvoir par Louis XIV*.

The remarkable scene in which Father Joly hears Mazarin's confession reveals much of the Cardinal's state of mind – we understand in a few seconds what he has been doing in his eighteen years as First Minister to the Crown. It is equally indicative of the political history of France in the latter half of the seventeenth century, showing the Church's influence on affairs of state and the country's shaky economic position. Equally, the scene in which the King

Stills: La Prise de pouvoir par Louis XIV – *the king gets up and visits the dying Mazarin.*

tries on suits and wigs, with his tailor, is not there entirely in the interests of documentary precision. It may show the dress of the period and all that, but it also provides both insight into Louis XIV's character – he orders more 'imposing' wigs to make up for his lack of height – and the implementation of an idea, the development of which is at the centre of the film. The idea is of imposing upon the rebellious members of the nobility a system of dress and manners complicated enough to assure Louis' control of them – a very serious political decision, in fact. As in *Vanina Vanini*,

the facts about a period are shown through characters in their actual setting, although there the process of analysis took second place to the demands of a fictional plot. *La Prise de pouvoir par Louis XIV* is essay rather than novel, description becomes narration and the subject is taken straight, free from any limitation: a study on the technique of a *coup d'état*. This *coup d'état* took place over a fairly long period in history – from the death of Mazarin in 1661 until 1682, the year of Louis XIV's installation at Versailles. It has been compressed, by a considerable feat, into the length of a normal

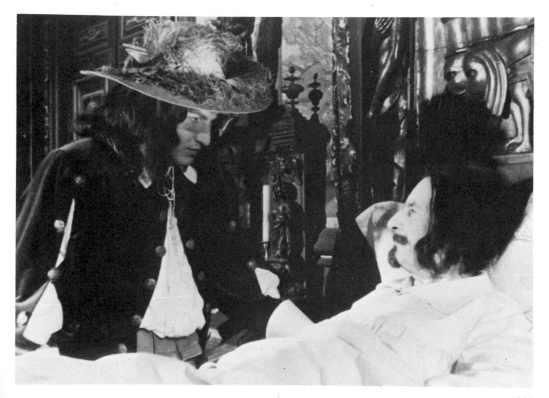

film (whereas *Era notte a Roma, Viva l'Italia!* and *Vanina Vanini*, which confined themselves to shorter segments of history, lasted respectively 145 minutes, 120 minutes and 130 minutes). Attention is nevertheless paid to all Louis XIV's reforms, despite the suppression of a scene in which the King reviewed the pensions granted to writers: Molière, Corneille, Racine, Boileau and La Fontaine were all under his patronage.

Scenes are chosen, therefore, for their informative value, not for any alleged dramatic weight, and those which would not add to the clarity of the account are quite simply omitted. This is why we do not see Mazarin's funeral, or the journey of the court to Nantes, the seat of the steward Fouquet, where the King arranges the meeting of his Cabinet. But this playing down of drama does not imply any rejection of spectacle: it is significant that the singular piece of *mise-en-scène* with which Louis XIV surrounds Fouquet's arrest should be shown in every detail, and that an exact account should be given of the functioning of the palace kitchens and the banquet ritual. This is like a religious ceremony or play. Unlike the political orators who turn into balalaika players in *October*, or the dismembered cattle that confront the Italian soldiers on their way to the defeat at Custozza in *Senso* (to take examples from two well known 'historical' films), these scenes in *La Prise de pouvoir par Louis XIV* have not the slightest satirical or allegorical significance. The point is merely to show logically how the King developed his method of sophisticated *mise-en-scène* as the means of taking power. The whole operation of the government and the court is changed into *mise-en-scène*. The simple fact of not being familiar with it – witness Vardes, the exiled nobleman – amounts to not existing in the eyes of the King. *La prise de pouvoir par Louis XIV* is about the concept of spectacle, as well as being a historical essay.

The King is not seen at the beginning, but becomes omnipresent by the end. His conquest of the screen is, therefore, only the image of his conquest of the court, that is, of his world. The initial lack of organisation, with confusion in the palace suggested by the servants and courtiers running back and forth, is turned into the dazzlingly conducted system of the royal banquet, which is in itself a symbol of triumph, by the conscious exercise of Louis' will. At the same time the muted colours of the beginning change into the brilliant tones that characterise the end. Here we can see the structure of the film: when Louis' *mise-en-scène* attains perfection, the assumption of power is complete. But after walking in the gardens of Versailles, the King withdraws to his private quarters, strips off his finery – gives up his performance – and anxiously meditates on La Rochefoucauld's maxim: '*Le soleil ni la mort ne se peuvent regarder fixement.*' Louis XIV is presented as a touching mixture of the urge to power and real timidity, in this he surprisingly fits the pattern of Rossellini characters. He has carried out his *coup d'état* at the price of complete loneliness. When he again becomes simply an individual, he seems to realise the fragility of all he has built up, to realise his weakness, in spite of his intellectual superiority to the flabby courtiers, to realise that others will put an end to the enterprise he has begun. Everything is fleeting, as it is in *India*. The ideas we have obtained must always be subject to question; the last word is never said. Yet again, the need not to pass judgement is stressed.

To see in every detail a reflection of the whole, to see in every gesture a sign of the times – these aims, accomplished here with such consistency, were detectable much earlier in Rossellini's work. Like *Paisà* in 1948, *Viaggio in Italia* in 1953 and *India* in 1958, *La Prise de pouvoir par Louis XIV* again won its bid to set a new standard of realism both in documentary and in

Still: La Prise de pouvoir par Louis XIV.

the cinema, generally. From now on, 'historical realism' acquires a new meaning. Through his compulsive need to teach and to learn, Rossellini surpassed the fumbling experiment of *L'età del ferro. La Prise de pouvoir par Louis XIV* makes earlier historical films look antiquated and opens the way to new and promising developments. It sheds further light on the director's decision to abandon theatrical films and demonstrates his faithful adherence to the plan of action

established in 1963:
'History, through teaching visually, can evolve on its own ground rather than evaporate into dates and names. Abandoning the usual litany of battle, it can surrender to its social, economic and political determinants. It can build, not on fantasy, but on historical knowledge, situations, costumes, atmospheres, and men who had historical significance and helped the social developments by which we live today. Some characters then, considered from a psychological viewpoint can, through their human qualities, become the embodiments of action.'

La Lotta del l'uomo per la sua sopravvivenza

A documentary in twelve episodes on man's struggle to survive, his war against death and the current possibility of universal suicide. The series extends from cave dwellers to modern journeys into space.

At the end of the Neolithic period, a woman and a little girl watch, fascinated, as a loaf of bread is cooking. This almost abstract shape, inert a few moments earlier, swells, changes shape and assumes a strange appearance of life, which is nevertheless the work of human hands. It is a very short scene, and only an infinitesimal part of the huge complex of *La Lotta dell'uomo per la sua sopravvivenza*, which was originally split up into twelve episodes, each lasting 90 minutes, though they have all since been edited down to an hour. But the scene says a lot more about the character of primitive man than many long explanations; it presents a simple and moving example of man's earliest creations. The synthetical power of Rossellini's imagination is such that he can reach the most abstract ideas by starting from very concrete examples.

Man's discovery of his own potentialities grows boundlessly: he covers himself with the skin of a boar to go bear hunting, uses camouflage while hunting ducks, learns to work metal and builds a pyramid. He also understands the implications of the decree proclaimed by a mediaeval overlord to the assembled vassals and thus wins a first bid for freedom. Rossellini's treatment of this scene is characteristic. A tracking shot explores the crowd and settles on one peasant who is explaining the meaning of the edict to his fellows: the nobleman is short of funds and wants to take hard-earned money from the people in order to get back to the Crusades. As in the banquet scene in *La Prise de pouvoir par Louis XIV*, the importance of the camera-movement is not aesthetic, but moral: it seeks to apprise us of a political fact. At the opening of an early university, in the thirteenth century, a lecturer claims that 'Mystery is failing to know.' *La Lotta dell'uomo per la sua sopravvivenza*, then, is a chronicle of man's intelligence.

The reconstruction of the ceremonies performed by matriarchal tribes combines simplicity and beastliness. The queen follows up a ritual dance and an eloquent dialogue of glances by sacrificing her husband to complete the fertility cycle in the Autumn. When she stands up, the camera position emphasises her pregnancy; one life goes on from another in a confluence, the earthly with the divine (symbolised respectively by the plough and the moon). The nobleman goes off to the Crusades, leaving his wife alone. The abandoned wife's eye lights on the first minstrel to appear, who is able only to immortalise her in the empty poetic impulse of 'courtly love'. But although many desires remain unsatisfied, the wandering minstrels, who scale mountains and visit widely varying places, prove a rich source of information, in touch with a world hitherto undreamed of. In an extension of the treatment attempted in *L'Età del ferro*, the simplest action is shown to have unexpected consequences and various degrees of repercussion; each gesture becomes a sign. The aim is to analyse as well as show. The method of which traces were already apparent in *Era notte a Roma* is developing into an increasingly coherent system.

During a fertility rite, the queen bathes in a waterfall – a perfect image of the integration of humans with nature. The juggler-minstrels play with apples, use water from the river for cooling wine and perform surprising acrobatics. These actions do not aspire to scientific accuracy, any more than they yield to the picturesque; their choice is part of the deliberate attempt at recapturing the atmosphere of an age. As they go on their way the jugglers meet a prisoner who is to be dismembered in a nearby village 'for the people's amusement' despite the fact that, as one of his guards admits, he has committed no crime – an image characteristic of mediaeval violence. The atmosphere comes over purely through actions. The arrival of the emissaries to announce to the village the lord's decree is reminiscent of Breughel, with gaudily coloured figures silhouetted against the snow, but the idea is not to reconstruct paintings. The appearance comes from the play between real elements, real costumes and real landscape. Similarly, in *La Prise de pouvoir par Louis XIV*, painstakingly authentic costumes and sets gave the appearance of pictures by Louis le Nain or Philippe de Champaigne, without implying any intentions in this direction.

The authenticity is embodied in gestures (the nobleman puts on his clothes before setting out for the Holy Land in a scene like that of the King's awakening in *La Prise de pouvoir par Louis XIV*) and actions: building a chariot, shoeing an ox, waterproofing fabrics, constructing windmills (copied from the Arabs), processing minerals. All are portrayed as accurately as possible and presented as documents of a logical development. *La Lotta dell'uomo per la sua sopravvivenza* is the result of the combined efforts of *L'Età del ferro* and *La Prise de pouvoir par Louis XIV*. The work is being shared by the same team: conception and production by Rossellini with the collaboration of his son as director, Renzo Rossellini Jr (who previously shot *L'Età del ferro* and

Still: La Lotta dell'uomo per la sua sopravvivenza.

some scenes for *La Prise de pouvoir par Louis XIV*). The division of labour is logical in view of the size of the project.

The series extends the attempt begun in *L'Età del ferro* to start a commentary on our civilisation, and continues to deepen the perspectives of a cinema that is, in the finest sense, didactic. A lesson has been learned from the success of *La Prise de pouvoir par Louis XIV*: there is no longer any more need for archive material, except for the NASA footage on space travel. Everything else is re-created in the same spirit as the earlier film, with a view to equalling its clarity and effectiveness of exposition.

When the whole series has been definitively edited, it will be possible to reach firm conclusions about the scope of the enterprise. In May 1970, after shooting *Socrate*, Rossellini is contemplating important changes in the last three episodes of *La Lotta dell'uomo per la sua sopravvivenza*, which have already been edited, to reveal more clearly a continuity between this series and *La Rivoluzione Industriale*, a series still in preparation. But it already seems clear that *L'Età del ferro*, *La Prise de pouvoir par Louis XIV* and *La Lotta dell'uomo per la sua sopravvivenza*, later joined by *Atti degli Apostoli* and *Socrate* (which will make up a triptych on classical civilisations to be completed with a film on Caligula), are the opening volleys in what appears to be a single, vast picture. It has an aim, unprecedented in the cinema or any other medium of communication, which goes towards granting Michelet's wish for 'a total reconstruction of Man's past'.

Atti degli Apostoli

I. In about A.D. 30 the Apostles announce on the day of Pentecost that the Lord has been among them. They call the pilgrims of Jerusalem to be baptised. Peter and John are twice arrested by the Sanhedrin for their work as witnesses of Christ, but are set free.

II. The Apostles start organising their community and choose new deacons. Stephen, one of the deacons, is stoned for disobeying the Mosaic Law on the Sabbath. His colleague, Philip, sets out for the desert and baptises an Ethiopian eunuch. Saul, persecutor of the Christians, is struck blind by the Lord on the way to Damascus.

III. Saul preaches his new faith in the synagogue at Damascus and is forced to escape from the town. Peter baptises a centurion, Cornelius, although it is forbidden for believers to enter the houses of Gentiles. Some years later, James the Greater attacks King Herod Agrippa for killing the starving crowd and is beheaded. Saul, who has been renamed Paul, makes his first mission journey from Antioch in Syria as far as Pisidian Antioch.

IV. Paul upholds the equality of all, circumcised and uncircumcised, in the eyes of the Lord. In A.D. 49 a meeting is called in Jerusalem to discuss the problem. It is decided not to bind converts to any obligations other than of refusing to eat meat sacrificed to idols and abstaining from fornication.

V. Paul arrives in Neapolis and preaches in Athens and Corinth on his first journey to Europe. On returning to Jerusalem in A.D. 57, he is arrested and sent to Rome for trial.

In the last sequence of *Atti degli Apostoli*, the aging Paul is visited in his prison at Rome by a young friend who is on a pilgrimage to

Still: La Lotta dell'uomo per la sua soprav-vivenza – *Stephenson's Rocket.*

Jerusalem. As they talk, Paul seems nostalgic for Jerusalem. He sends a message to a certain Carpus at Troas, asking him to send a cloak, because 'winter, is cold in Rome'. He speaks of the prison: 'I have lived in this room for two years'; 'imprisonment is pleasant'; 'you wouldn't think that I would be free to have visits from anyone who wants to come'; 'the Rome of the Caesars reaches right to my room'. He admits that he has failed: 'the Elders of the Synagogue have been coming since the first day and they left as they came, without believing. Here, as everywhere, most of the people of Israel still reject Messiah.' He admonishes fellow Jews in the prison at Rome: ' . . . thou bearest not the root, but the root thee.' [Romans XI, 18]. He ends by dictating a letter, in which he foretells: 'Men will be full of pride . . . There will come a time when they no longer take the words of truth. They will follow their own unhealthy tastes and go with masters they pretend to hear, going all the while away from charity, seeking myths.' He announces his own end – 'My blood is already poured as a libation,' – and publicly announces his faith: 'I have fought a good fight, I have finished my course. I have kept the faith.' [2 Timothy IV, 7.] And with his farewell, 'God be with thy spirit', he gives proof of his joy with a touching smile. It is perhaps the most beautiful moment in *Atti degli Apostoli*, and certainly the one which best expresses the spirit of this outstanding film.

This final sequence is shot in a single take which starts on a close-up of Paul's face and ends on another of him smiling; in between it shows the whole of the room that acts as his prison, the arrival of the Roman guard with the day's food and his conversation with a prisoner who suspects that the meat might have been sacrificed to idols (and thus forbidden to Jews), Paul's admonition to his fellow prisoners and the dictation of a letter to his brothers in Jerusalem. The Pancinor shifts unceasingly in and out with the same systematic precision as in *La prise de pouvoir par Louis XIV*, freely following the characters' movements, revealing the décor along with the action and, at all times, taking up the best position to see. The choosing of Matthew in place of the traitor Judas, the appearance of Peter and John among the crowd of pilgrims in Jerusalem on the day of Pentecost, the first meal together (a conscious repetition of the ceremony of the Last Supper), the appointment of the Greek-speaking deacons, the arrest of James outside Herod Agrippa's palace, the first great Council at Jerusalem and Paul's sermon in the night to the people of Corinth; telling and important moments in *Atti degli Apostoli*, are all filmed using this technique. The constant movement of the image, conveys the dialectical shift from individual to collective which shapes the whole film and reflects a spirit of enquiry – a physical search for the best perspective in which to consider the facts at any moment. The zoom out from a close up of Saul's face to Stephen's lifeless body is not merely *mise-en-scène*, but gives us to understand his responsibility in part for the young deacon's death. On the arrival of Paul and Silas at the Greek port of Neapolis, the camera tracks back without any dramatic purpose, but simply to give a general picture of the port and a clearer indication of where we are.

Almost every scene in *Atti degli Apostoli* was shot in the characteristic *plan-séquence*. There isn't any montage. Rossellini, putting the film together himself at his house in Rome, needed only to join up the ends of shots already 'edited' by the Pancinor in shooting. Even if the inward and outward movements place any emphasis on the actions shown, these are caught as they occur in their actual, unbroken order. It is precisely when the facts shown are of a purely didactic nature that there is cutting. The images of life in Jerusalem shown by Aristarcus to the Roman magistrate at the beginning of the film, and the images of Roman life shown to Paul by Christians of the city (which in both cases present historical, economic, social or religious facts), are always atonal and express little in themselves. They are intercut purely as illustration of the things being explained by the characters. The originality of these sequences lies in their remarkable lack of any claim to 'realism'. They are purely informative, like diagrams used in a treatise, or almost like slides illustrating a lecture. *Atti degli Apostoli*, then, completes the process of eliminating classical *mise-en-scène* which was begun in *L'Età del ferro*. So it seems quite rational that the same desire to find another level of discussion, to take a fresh look at reality, which implies a breakdown of the traditional structures of *mise-en-scène*, should lead Rossellini to re-invent the cinema: the image of Zachariah leading his caravan away to disappear on the horizon in the last section of *Atti degli Apostoli* could have come out of a western, the first organised form in the cinema.

During his enforced retirement at Rome, Paul begs his young visitor to ask a friend in Troas for his cloak; he dictates a letter sending greetings to his friends in Jerusalem and hoping Timothy will 'come to Rome before the winter'. The stress in *Atti degli Apostoli* is on the commonplace. Paul is recognised, while being shaved, by a passer-by at the Gate of the Temple in Jerusalem and is immediately arrested. James is simply taken to the city gate and beheaded without the least ceremony, watched by chance passers-by and herds of domestic animals; the camera merely zooms out very slowly to record his leading-out and execution. After the first meeting of the Council in Jerusalem to confront the threat to the young church of dissension among its members, Peter tells Paul the story of Hillel, who was challenged by a heathen to explain the whole law of Israel in the length of time a man can stay standing

Still: Atti degli Apostoli – *the Apostles' first supper together.*

on one leg. While he recounts this, Peter raises his leg, laughing. At times we again find the prodigious spontaneity of *Francesco. giullare di Dio,* and the very simplicity of the actions is almost in the realms of fantasy, for example, in the episode (shot by Renzo Rossellini Jr), when Philip meets the Ethiopian eunuch, or in the prayer inside an oven, where Syrian brethren show Paul and Barnabas that they have been called by the Holy Ghost to go out and preach

to the world (news which they receive with some trepidation), or in the surprising image of the gates of Jerusalem shutting with a frightful grinding noise, so that the slower disciples are forced to pass the night outside. The humility with which Paul asks for a cloak fits with the style of Rossellini, who is always attentive to the small gestures which can stir deep reverberations. But this detail – like the wonderful words of the Apostle – is merely taken from the Second Epistle to Timothy [2 Timothy, IV, 13], in the same way that the visit of the Bourbon generals to Garibaldi

appears in *Viva l'Italia!* just as recounted in Bandi's diary. This use of accurate and realistic sources gives substance to what might have been only reconstruction; lost events from a distant past come very close to us. In a surprising number of ways the treatment of Paul and Garibaldi is strikingly similar. Both of them bring quiet strength to their struggle for an ideal and receive the failure of their dreams with equal calm. Paul is also reminiscent of the two complementary characters of Salvatore in *Dov'è la libertà?* and Irene in *Europa '51*. Like Salvatore, he is the victim of unrighteous

Still: Atti degli Apostoli – *Stephen's body.*

bureaucracy and comes under police control in Rome. Like Irene, and in a way, like Pietro in *Vanina Vanini*, he finds his freedom in prison; in other words he only becomes free in the knowledge of the freedom he does not have. The treatment of Paul is very characteristic of Rossellini, but Stephen's martyrdom (there is a wonderful image of his body hanging from a dead tree, with his friends sitting in a circle some distance away), Paul's escape in a basket from persecution in Damascus, and the decapitation of James go back to the time of *Roma, città aperta* and *Paisà*. With Rossellini's talent for synthesis, it is clearly not accidental that his work for television should recall all his earlier films, as *L'Età del ferro* showed.

Paul's imprisonment in a room at Rome under the constant watch of a soldier is given in a simple five-minute sequence which none the less expresses two years of close confinement. The film shows none of the events following Paul's arrest in Jerusalem and described by Luke in the Acts of the Apostles: Paul's speech to the people; his committal for trial by Felix, the governor; his appearance before Agrippa. The Apostle's call as a Roman citizen for justice from Caesar is mentioned only in a single sentence by a chance observer of his departure from Caesarea. Paul's many missions and journeys are linked together in ellipses which sometimes abridge whole years. In spite of its great length, 5 hours 42 minutes, *Atti degli Apostoli* is a brutally elliptic film which goes straight to the essential. All the episodes seem indispensable for an understanding of the whole and time is spent only on events which are truly important; the Council at Jerusalem, for example, takes up almost the whole fourth chapter. However, the spectacular incidents of Paul's voyage to Rome, which give Luke's account the look of an early forerunner to the modern adventure novel, are omitted: there is nothing of the adventure film here. With the exception of Peter's healing the lame man at the gate of the Temple and the appearance of Jesus before Saul, the miracles of which Luke's account is full are forgotten. There is no mention of Herod Agrippa's death after having James beheaded, or the resurrection of Tabitha or the various manifestations of the Lord, the Holy Ghost, angels etc. The wondrous visitations and the Apostles' visions are quite simply recounted to friends as dreams, or to disciples as irresistible forces which drive Peter to Joppa, where the brethren had thought themselves abandoned (the image of a full moon significantly opens and ends this sequence), and Paul to Troas, in the direction of Europe.

So we remain in the realm of human behaviour. When Philip decides to go into the desert, he is inspired not by an angel, but by the death of Stephen. Paul always wants someone with him on his journeys, because he is subject to sudden illnesses (he arrives at Pisidia visibly shaking with fever) and he does not know how to speak to the wives of the Jews in Neapolis because he is not accustomed to it. The actors' faces are realistically rustic and as far away from typical movie hagiography as those of *Francesco, giullare di Dio*. The Ascension of Christ, which opens Luke's account, is not shown and we begin with a long account of the situation in Israel in A.D. 30. Thus we immediately see the Apostles' confusion in the absence of their master, their need to obey the compulsion to bear witness to an idea, whose significance was quite beyond them, and their development as people. *Atti degli Apostoli*, then, does not take the narrative form in which the events were set down by Luke, but that of a logical report, arranged in a rigorous progression of cause and effect. James's martyrdom is a very clear example of this. There is a great famine in the surrounding countryside; the people attack a cart carrying flour into the royal palace; the soldiers massacre the rioters; James closes the eyes of one of their victims and turns on those responsible; he is arrested and Herod Agrippa decides that he is both an *agent provocateur* (which displeases the Romans) and a follower of Jesus (which infuriates the Sanhedrin). Given that his death would be a gesture of political wisdom, pleasing both groups, he condemns James to decapitation. *Atti degli Apostoli* therefore centres on the consequences of an idea in the hearts of a small group of men.

It is while he is imprisoned at Rome that Paul makes a statement of his faith. Because of his defence of the Gentiles, the Jews of Jerusalem demand that he pray in the Temple, as public proof of his adherence to the Law of Moses, although this means for him a danger of arrest, which inevitably happens. It is significant that the speech made by Stephen to the Sanhedrin as reported in Luke's text is translated into practical action. Although the law expressly forbids it, Stephen distributes food on the Sabbath to Christians who are in need. It is not enough for him to repeat the words of Jesus, 'the life of a man is worth more than the Sabbath', which he quotes before the tribunal. He has to put them into practice and be stoned to death for it. The Apostles' testimony, like that of the little monks in *Francesco, giullare di Dio* has to take effect in actions, not words. Nicodemus sells all his possessions to help the survival of the growing Christian community. Philip decides to join the group at the moment of greatest danger, when Peter and John have just been arrested by the Sanhedrin, and baptises the Ethiopian eunuch. Peter baptises Cornelius the centurion, although he is forbidden, as a Jew, to go into the house of a Gentile. James denounces Herod's cruelty. Silas baptises the Greek lady, Lydia. Paul repeats the sermon on the mount to the crowd at Corinth and goes to prison as a proof of his faith. Zachariah works as an honest merchant and teaches travellers in the caravan he leads to pray. Each acts on his own initiative, according to his own conscience in the situation he has to confront, knowing nothing of the actions of his brethren, so that each act becomes an extension of the same idea.

Each act also becomes a symbol of the times. It is only necessary to consider the spurious pythoness of Apollo at Neapolis, and the feeble attitude of the city authorities towards the injuries suffered by Paul and Silas, to understand the decadence of Greece, by now merely a colony of Rome. On his journey to Athens, Paul meets a passer-by and asks the way: in answer, he is told the tale of Achilles and the tortoise. At one of the stops, the travellers in the caravan discuss their problems and beliefs – the need to send goods to Egypt because a comet indicates a rise in prices, the complications incurred by purchasing a Jewish slave, the cure for falling off one's horse, the years needed to attain the seventh heaven, the loss of a harvest – passing references to all the ideas and superstitions of the age. Facts are not discussed, simply confronted. On the day of Pentecost, two wise men foretell the future (one reads it in the oil, the other tells it with sticks) as the Apostles appear, exhorting all those present to come and be baptised. The friends' simple meal together, where a cup is passed from hand to hand in a wonderful physical expression of the concept of communion, contrasts with the sacrifice of a sheep at the Temple. The idea is, then, to give an objective view of life in Israel from all angles, and the result is a huge documentary on this life.

Paul does not seem idle, imprisoned in his room at Rome. He writes, attempts to strengthen the ties between the many Christian communities and meditates. The witness he bears is inseparable from his ordinary work. When he stays with Manaen in Syria, he is seen pressing clay with his feet while he explains to a woman that Jesus preached against discrimination. In Pisidia he helps the weaver with his work, as he talks about Christ's resurrection. At the beginning of *Atti degli Apostoli*, Aristarcus the Greek explains to the Roman magistrate newly arrived in Jerusalem how important work is to the Jews: 'You can understand a lot about them by carefully watching them at work. Look at their concentration . . . as if they are delighted and wholly taken up with what they're doing.' Like the Franciscans in *Francesco, giullare di Dio,* they seem to look upon work as a means of communicating with God. Zachariah goes on working as a merchant because the Lord has taught him to be honest and not to change his job. The Apostles never cease being active throughout the film. They bake bread in the courtyard of Mark's house, where the members of the community gather together when Peter and John come out of prison. They also bake

Still: Atti degli Apostoli – *Peter is brought before the Sanhedrin. Right –. Paul.*

the slabs of clay on which Stephen has made a note of offerings received. Ananias is working in an oven when he hears the call to go and meet Saul. John and Peter put up a tent in the olive grove before the gathering. This manual work has more than purely documentary value, since it is a visible sign of the Apostles' faith. In all probability, the sight of an absolute forest of jars through the gates of Jerusalem is intentional, visually characterising the city; work itself and its results, then, become the image of the city.

During Paul's confinement in his room in

Still: Atti degli Apostoli – *the pilgrims are baptised in the brook Cedron.*

Rome, one is sadly conscious of the absence of nature, omnipresent elsewhere in the film from the valleys Paul and Barnabas pass through in Antioch to the Mount of Olives where the Christian communities hold their first full council – not to mention the deserts Zachariah's caravan crosses. In fact, practically all the conflicts in *Atti degli Apostoli* take place in the open air, in an absolute communion between man and nature. Saul is placed near a stream

when he is blinded by the vision of Jesus; after washing his hands and bathing his head and face, he is baptised with water drawn by Ananias from Judas's well and regains his sight. Later, as Paul, at Troas in the course of his first voyage to Europe, he speaks of the sea 'which embraces the whole world, just as the

Holy Ghost embraces all of creation.' Water is of prime importance, from the brook, Cedron, where Peter baptises the pilgrims on the day of Pentecost, to the sprinkling in baptism, recalled so movingly by Philip – 'the rain which fell on them was the same as that which fell on me' – before the Council and including the lake by which Zachariah's caravan rests. Water forms the strongest symbolic motif in *Atti degli Apostoli* and stresses its religious character. (Many acts of cleansing, an important ritual for the Jewish people, are seen.) The fifth episode deals with the contrast between Paul's prison at Rome and the freedom of his missionary journeys in Europe. This freedom is illustrated in a counterpoint of images showing birds in flight at significant moments, immediately before Paul's arrival at Athens and at Corinth. Their connection is particularly strong when the Apostle arrives at Miletus and decides to return to Jerusalem, where he will be arrested. This is almost the only burst of lyricism in which the film indulges; all the emotion in it is firmly based on the logic and clarity of its argument.

The Roman soldier's respect for the religious beliefs of Jewish prisoners, and Paul's reference to the indifference met by his words in the Rome synagogue, are among the instances in the last sequence of *Atti degli Apostoli* of attitudes aroused by the Apostles' statement of their faith. Caiaphas quickly leaves the cell in which Peter and John spend their first imprisonment, when John asks if he should obey him rather than God himself. Just as Paul's statement in Athens contests the intellectual authority of the Sophists, so the questioning of Caiaphas's religious authority also implies a challenge to his political authority from the moment that the absolute religious power of the Temple – as Aristarcus explains to the Roman magistrate – becomes identified with political power, a power which the Roman prefect and Herod Agrippa both respect. The uproar caused in Jerusalem by the Apostles' first public appearance on the day of Pentecost stirs the Roman garrison to action. 'A pointless argument about the nature of divinity,' Aristarcus points out, has immediate political repercussions. Scarcely have the Roman soldiers arrived in Jerusalem at the very beginning of the film, when they have reluctantly to put away their standards. The magistrate is immediately warned by the prefect in person: 'Of all the cities in the Empire, this is the hardest to govern.' Aristarcus advises the newcomer to wear a toga without distinguishing marks when visiting the city, to avoid incidents with the Jews. It is for the sake of the threatened authorities, both religious and secular, that 'political wisdom' leads the King to condemn James to be beheaded. Because his power is threatened by the quarrels of the Christians in Rome, the Emperor Claudius orders the expulsion of Roman Jews. On the other hand, while the caravan is resting, Bethel suggests to Zachariah that it was a betrayal for the Saviour to hope to bring salvation to all people, when he should have come as liberator of the Jews, who were downtrodden by the weight of Roman domination. This accusation was brought up, too, in Nicholas Ray's *King of Kings* (1960) – it is interesting to note the similarities in direction between the slaughter of patriots rioting against the Roman soldiers in this film and that of the starving crowd in the third episode of *Atti degli Apostoli*. The pacifist preaching of the Christians was very well suited to the interests of the Romans as invaders: 'They won't change the world', the magistrate remarks with satisfaction after the stir caused by the appearance of Peter and John on the evening after Pentecost. Without any desire to do so, and in spite of their humility, the Apostles had a decisive influence on Hebrew nationalism and the political conflicts of the time. By destroying the concept expressed by Aristarcus, that 'from his birth, a man belongs to a system from which he is completely unable to escape without risking the most terrible punishment', they give a new meaning to the word Freedom. 'Jesus will restore his Father's Kingdom when he has destroyed all authority, all rule and all power', Paul explains while working with the weaver at Pisidia. *Atti degli Apostoli* therefore sets out to give an impartial account of a revolution.

Surrounded by other Jewish prisoners in his room at Rome, Paul preaches that all are equal before the Lord. Throughout his work, he is not content to preach this conviction without practising it. He decides that Manaen has committed no sin in leaving his new-born son uncircumcised. He allows the baptism of the Greek, Lydia, at Neapolis. The Greek members of the newly-formed Christian community are the first to feel the discrimination implicit in Mosaic religion; they are abandoned by their Jewish brethren and their claim for assistance leads Peter to press for the election of seven Greek-speaking deacons, one of whom is Stephen. The young deacon loses his life, convinced like Jesus that 'the Sabbath was made for man, not man for the Sabbath.' His religious beliefs, then, lead him to a new social awareness. Each through his own experience, the Apostles are forced by charity to respect human beings as such: Philip explains a difficult point of the scriptures to the eunuch and then baptises him, Peter asks the centurion to stand up, saying, 'I myself also am a man' [Acts X, 26], Paul and Barnabas kiss the hands of the shepherd they meet on the way to Pisidia. Paul later tells Peter, 'Jesus spoke to me on the way to Damascus. And in a moment all the force of the law . . . and pride . . fell from my heart.' But it is not simply because of this that Paul understands 'those who have not grown up in the tradition of Moses cannot accept the laws and customs of our people.' Manaen tells Paul

'Antioch is not like Jerusalem,' referring to the free and spontaneous integration of Christians and Gentiles in Antioch, a region through which caravans pass from east to west, exchanging information and letting ideas and customs intermingle. That is to say, it has the sort of culture that Paul gathers on his travels (in Corinth he shows his respect for Socrates and Plato) learning concrete facts and extending the vision with which he confronts various problems. With the respect for fellow beings comes the awareness of personal dignity: Silas protests when he and Paul are imprisoned without the trial to which they are entitled as Roman citizens and, when he is arrested in Jerusalem, Paul will not submit to scourging without previous judgement according to Roman law.

In the film, the Apostles baptise an Ethiopian eunuch, a Roman centurion and a Greek lady. The ecumenical nature of their Christianity was bound to seem completely revolutionary to the Hebraic society of their time. It went so far as to challenge the social structure, which was founded on a system of many castes – Pharisees, Sadducees, Essenes, Hellenists, Herodians, etc., as Aristarcus indicates – and the great pride in the sacred ritual of circumcision: 'the symbol in flesh of the agreement they [the Jews] have made with God. It is their exclusive privilege, like a magic circle that excludes everyone else on earth.' (The importance of the film's didactic introduction cannot be overemphasised here. It gives the essentials of the conflict and gives overall dramatic coherence to the argument by allowing us to grasp the full implications of the Apostles' revolution. Where *Francesco giullare di Dio* appeals to our intuition and sensitivity, *Atti degli Apostoli* uses our reason and intelligence.) The badly-needed equality scandalises the rabbis of Jerusalem, Damascus and Antioch, preoccupied as they are with following the letter of the law, and meets with a flat refusal. All the Jews who are not Christians leave when Zachariah ends his prayers by the lake at dusk with the Lord's Prayer. Even the young church is threatened by a schism: Paul's conversion and his ideas of integration are greeted with distrust and hostility. Although he has the approval of one of the Elders, Peter is blamed for entering the house of a pagan. Zachariah will not share Paul's communal meal with the Syrian converts, because he believes that it would be a crime according to Mosaic Law. It is to deal with these problems that representatives of all the Christian communities meet in Jerusalem, nineteen years after the death of Jesus. In spite of the possibility that the Council will break up before it has begun,

Still: Atti degli Apostoli – *Paul takes a communal meal with converts in Antioch.*

– one group refuse to admit Titus, a disciple who is uncircumcised – the Apostles succeed in winning round those who are doubtful by their faith and make the point that all are equal before God. (But doubts survive: Paul is arrested as a result of demands that he make a public statement in the Temple.) *Atti degli Apostoli* is thus presented as a historical analysis which documents the appearance of the first democratic society after Christ.

In the letter to Timothy, dictated under house arrest at Rome, Paul, who has aged noticeably, draws up the balance-sheet of his activity. His words express a sudden awareness of time: twenty-five years have passed since his conversion, a lengthy cycle. Yet the logical sequence of events as well as the immediacy of their presentation – at the beginning of the film, Aristarcus takes the magistrate along the Way of the Cross and shows him the still visible

stains of Jesus's blood – would make its passage almost imperceptible, if it were not for the references to time provided in the confrontations between the characters: the discussion between Bethel and Zachariah, for example, covers twenty years of political conflict in Israel. Paul's request that Timothy come to Rome before winter, now emphasises the Apostle's complete solitude as well as announcing his approaching death. Although there are a few things to be grateful for, the baptism of Lydia and the confident faith of a few Athenians, Paul's life has settled into what looks like failure: he has had to escape from Damascus and Pisidia; he has been beaten in Neapolis for unmasking the soothsayer of Apollo; he has been made to appear ridiculous by Sophists in the Areopagus, he has been arrested at Jerusalem, he is a prisoner in Rome and he observes the inevitable divisions springing up among Christians everywhere. But Paul remains calm. When he reaches Neapolis on his first journey to Europe, one of his hosts explains the particular attractions of Philippi, where Brutus and Cassius, Caesar's murderers, were beaten. The Apostle merely declares, 'This is where the story of the Caesars begins. The story of Man began somewhere else.' He greets the brethren at Rome very much as representative and spokesman of an idea. Unlike the other Apostles, Paul – who explains to the Sophists in Athens his obsession with the problem of total knowledge – realises fully the import of the revolution his testimony will require and attains absolute wisdom. He remains joyful in spite of the failure of his missionary work; there is failure, too, in Bethel's bitter words to Zachariah, although they signify that the Christian faith has survived through the reigns of several emperors – Tiberius, Caligula, Claudius, Nero. When he is free, Paul is happy because he 'journeys to share my joy with all men in every land' (as he says on entering Pisidia); in prison, Paul maintains his perfect joy because he has understood that his cause was just. (So, before his death, did Socrates, the subject of Rossellini's next film.)

The last sequence of *Atti degli Apostoli* begins with a close-up of Paul's earnest face and ends with a similar close-up. He repeats the words of the psalm, 'Jesusalem, Jerusalem! Thou art like the deer crouching in the hills. Thy name is as loud as a trumpet call, but as soft as the song of flutes' which we have already heard at the start of the film when a group of pilgrims on the horizon come down towards the city of Jerusalem. This *plan-séquence* thus appears cyclic, but then, so is the whole film. The precise and informative account of Jerusalem in the first chapter, corresponds exactly with that of Rome in the last. The film also describes a vast temporal span – thirty-one years – about which there is provided a great body of information, political, religious, industrial, economic, historical and social, interrelated with the activity of the Apostles. Paul does not appear at all in the beginning of the film, but imperceptibly develops into the central figure after the end of the first chapter. This is entirely appropriate, since, as he tells the Jewish shepherd in Pisidia, 'my name, before, was Saul; now I am Paul. My name has changed like my heart.' Paul seems, then, to be a symbol of the complete change that *Atti degli Apostoli* is meant to chronicle. The film documents the decadence of Israel, Greece and Rome, while describing and analysing the early growth of a new society. Paul is the visible sign of both, in that he represents the passing world and announces the world to come. *Atti degli Apostoli* therefore attempts the complete synthesis of a world, perhaps unlike any previously ventured by a film-maker. In spite of the bitterness of the conclusion, it ends on a note of joy. However hesitantly, Man has written a new chapter in his history. The revolution has already begun.

Socrate

In 404 B.C, after his conquest of Athens, the Spartan Lysander orders the city fortifications to be torn down and imposes the Oligarchy of Thirty Tyrants. Socrates' unpopularity increases because of the repressive use Critias, the philosopher's former student, makes of his power. Critias commands Socrates and four other citizens to arrest Cleon of Salamis, but the philosopher refuses to carry out his order. His life is saved, indirectly, by the intervention of patriots led by Thrasybulus who overthrow the tyrants and subsequently restore the democracy in 403 B.C. But Socrates continues to arouse hostility among his fellow citizens. In 399 B.C. Meletus, Anytus and Lycon accuse the philosopher of being a threat to society. Socrates refuses Lysias' help and resolves to carry out his own defence at his trial. Despite his innocence, he is condemned to death. The execution is postponed for a month because the sacred ship is late in its yearly journey from Delos. Socrates refuses this opportunity to escape. When the ship comes in, he drinks hemlock and dies among his friends.

The film opens as the ramparts of Athens are broken down with a battering ram. This is a visible sign of the defeat that the Athenians have just suffered at the hands of the Spartans and their Lacedemonian allies. Then, straight away, we witness the wealthier citizens' re-actions to the establishment of tyranny. Hyperides holds Alcibiades responsible for the calamity. Theophrastus, however, upholds him as a great general and lays the blame on the Athenians' strategy. Phocion reminds them that the Spartans have been merciful in preventing the complete destruction of the city which the Thebans demanded. Significantly, this dis-cussion takes place during vast feasting, while outside, Athens looks deserted and the people

are starving after the long siege. Halfway through the film, after an encounter with a singer-poet, Socrates is challenged, in the agora, by an actor who recalls Aristophanes's portrayal of him in 'The Clouds', reciting a dialogue which parodies Socrates' reasoning. This scene, shot with a Pancinor in a single, long take, like the rest of the film, goes further than simple revival of the atmosphere of the period, however vivid, and 'present-tense'; it shows what the people made of Socrates' teaching, along with the religious and political hostility it aroused, for which the philosopher had later to face trial. Rossellini's concern is, therefore, to show all possible aspects of a particular historical situation with an extraordinary feeling of urgency.

When Socrates goes with Crito and his followers to watch the sacrifice of a cock to Asclepius, he questions the meaning of death and more or less predicts his own approaching end. This scene sheds light, psychologically, on the character, but it also records the nature and importance of religion in Athens. The lodging of complaints on the gateway of the Basileus including Meletus's claim against Socrates, the system of choosing the jury of five-hundred-and-one needed for the trial, and the legislative ritual which is set out in accurate detail, all record for us the Athenians' idea of law. Lysias' speech in defence and Socrates' meetings with Hippias and Euthyphron provide a good account of the art of eloquence and various aspects of philosophical thought in Greece. The continual shifting between the general and the particular is intended to make *Socrate* the chronicle of a civilisation, as well as of a particular personal experience, in much the same way as *La Prise de pouvoir par Louis XIV* and *Atti degli Apostoli*. This approach seems typical of Rossellini and has emerged as a deliberate method of exposition.

Socrates goes shopping in the market and

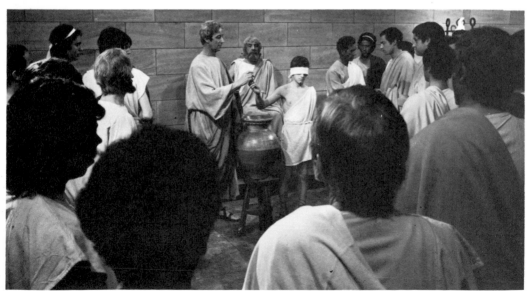

pays for an octopus with a coin which he has been keeping in his mouth – again we get the same careful re-creation of the past through the most simple, commonplace details. But, again, this action seems to take the form of: a) historical information – Socrates keeps his money in his mouth because the clothes of the period did not have pockets; b) a sign of his humility – 'I do not dress like a prince', he tells a lout who has been abusing him – the first words we hear him speak; c) an indication of character – the philosopher came to make some purchases, but has forgotten what he meant to do. The whole film is notable for this kind of synthesis: when Socrates arrives home, his

children are playing with Hoplite armour, the only remaining souvenir of their father's past career as a soldier.

Before saying goodbye to Xanthippe and the children in prison, Socrates rubs his ankle which has been bruised by the chains. This detail is taken straight from 'Phaedo'; there is the same preference for true details as in *Viva l'Italia!* and *Atti degli Apostoli. Socrate* was developed in the way now customary in Rossellini's films, starting from Plato's Dialogues and filling them out with information of, for example, a political, social, economic or religious nature about Athenian life. 'Euthyphron', the 'Apology', 'Crito' and 'Phaedo' – which deal with the last days of Socrates – make up the greater part of the film, but considerable liberties are taken with the remaining Dialogues. All that is used of 'Phaedrus', for instance, is the exhortation on rhetoric (which Socrates

Stills: Socrate. Opposite – Socrates is ordered by the oligarchy not to talk to the young; the drawing of lots for new magistrates. Below – Socrates learns he has been accused; Xanthippe.

delivers to Lycias on the subject of his defence oration) and the fable about King Thamus of Egypt and the demon, Teuth, in a discussion of the superiority of the spoken over the written word. A scene of Socrates' meeting with Hippias is included, like another with Lycias, to bring out the different standards which separated the philosopher from the Sophists. This is an acceptable method, when you consider that Plato made no claim to describe scenes which actually took place, but was merely illustrating the thoughts of his mentor. (The value of other changes is more arguable. Xanthippe, about whom almost nothing factual is known, is not given the shrewish nature tradition demands, but is treated with great warmth. It is a reasonable view, for our historical knowledge suggests as strongly as the film that Socrates must have been a trying husband. Nevertheless, my feeling is that Rossellini's effort to redeem Xanthippe was too strong and made her too sympathetic. However, it is a natural decision for a director who has made a point of not passing judgement on his characters.)

In view of the source, it is only logical that the finest part of *Socrate* should be the dialogue; this brings to its conclusion a tendency already obvious in *La Prise de pouvoir par Louis XIV*. (Which paradoxically leads Rossellini to bring cinematic *mise-en-scène* close to theatrical production as he understands it – as 'a simple job of arrangement, of making clear what is in the text'; this text has now become the main topic of his films. It is worth adding at this point that the shooting script of *Socrate*, which was rewritten every day, contained only the dialogue column, as Rossellini hates any written instructions of *mise-en-scène*.) As a vehicle of reasoning, the dialogue was Socrates' natural means of expressing himself, since he never wrote down any of his ideas. In the film we see him make use of his taste for irony: 'If I am

kicked by an ass, I do not get angry. It is hard to bring asses to justice,' he tells one of the crowd who shows surprise at his mildness. When Xanthippe complains in the prison that he is going to die unjustly, Socrates asks, 'Would you be happier to see me die guilty?' But the dialogue also sets down the method of Socratic reasoning, which develops in a constant exchange of question and answer, on the subjects, in the film, of madness, eloquence, death, injustice, politics, rhetoric, beauty, knowledge and the immortality of the soul. In taking as its theme the first logically organised philosophy in the history of man, which gave rise through Plato and Aristotle to the science of logic, *Socrate* seems to be as concerned with spoken phrases as with a defence and illustration of language.

Socrate was a project in Rossellini's mind for twenty years; it is the first film for television that he has shot without the help of his son, Renzo. In a traditional sense, it is his most personal work since *Illibatezza*, his last film for the cinema. It is not inconsistent, since the philosopher, set on stating his moral code in actions as well as words, defiantly solitary, and electing to die innocent in prison to prove his freedom as a man, is revealed as being like Garibaldi, Louis XIV or Paul, a very Rossellini character. Again, disturbing similarities can be found between the philosopher and the director: they share the same love of logic, the same independence and obstinacy; both have greatly influenced young people and both have awakened comparable religious and political hostility. Taking this game further than it can reasonably go, perhaps someone might venture to say that the contribution of one to philosophy has been equalled by the other in film making . . . But it is easier to stress Rossellini's insistence during the 'sixties and his current phase of didactic cinema that the greatest of virtues is knowledge – exactly as Socrates expounded.

Filmography

1936: DAPHNE
Directed by Roberto Rossellini. (short)

1938: PRELUDE A L'APRES-MIDI D'UN FAUNE
Directed by Roberto Rossellini. (short)

1938: *Luciano Serra, Pilota*
Directed by Goffredo Alessandrini. Written by Roberto Rossellini and Goffredo Alessandrini. Supervision by Vittorio Mussolini.

1939: FANTASIA SOTTOMARINA
Directed by Roberto Rossellini. Production: Incom. Photographed by Rodolfo Lombardi. Music by Edoardo Micucci. (short)

1939: IL TACCHINO PREPOTENTE
Directed by Roberto Rossellini. Photographed by Mario Bava. (short)

1939: LA VISPA TERESA
Directed by Roberto Rossellini. Photographed by Mario Bava. (short)

1941: IL RUSCELLO DI RIPASOTTILE
Directed by Roberto Rossellini. Production: Excelsior, SACI. (short)

1941: LA NAVE BIANCA
Directed by Roberto Rossellini. Production: Scalera, Centro Cinematografico del Ministero della Marina. Written by Francesco De Robertis and Roberto Rossellini. Story and supervision by Francesco De Robertis. Photographed by Emanuele Caracciolo. Décor by Amletto Benetti. Edited by Eraldo Da Roma. Music by Renzo Rossellini. 77 minutes.
With non-professional actors.

1942: UN PILOTA RITORNA
Directed by Roberto Rossellini. Production: ACI. Written by Michelangelo Antonioni, Rosario Leone, Massimo Mida, Gherardo Gherardi, Ugo Betti, Margherita Maglione, Roberto Rossellini. Photographed by Vincenzo Seratrice. Edited by Eraldo Da Roma. Music by Renzo Rossellini. 87 minutes.
With Massimo Girotti (the pilot), Michela Belmonte (the girl), Gaetano Masier, Piero Lulli, Giovanni Valdambrini, Nino Brendello, Elvira Betrone, Jole Tinta, Piero Palmerini, officers and men of the Italian Air Force.

1942: *I Tre Aquilotti*
Directed by Mario Mattoli. Music by Renzo Rossellini. Roberto Rossellini is said to have collaborated on this film.

1943: L'UOMO DELLA CROCE
Directed by Roberto Rossellini. Production: Continentalcine-Cines. Written by Asvero Gravelli, Alberto Consiglio, G. D'Alicandro and Roberto Rossellini from a story by Asvero Gravelli. Photographed by Guglielmo Lombardi. Décor by Gastone Medin. Music by Renzo Rossellini. 88 minutes.
With Alberto Tavazzi (the priest), Roswita Schmidt, Zoia Weneda, Doris Hild, Antonio Marietti, Piero Pastore, Aldo Capacci, Attilio Detesio, F. Castellani, M. Tanzi.

1943: *L'Invasore*
Directed by Nino Giannini. Written by Gherardo Gherardi, Nino Giannini, Roberto Rossellini. Supervised by Roberto Rossellini.

1943: DESIDERIO
Directed by Roberto Rossellini, Marcello Pagliero. Production: Sovrania, SAEIR. Written by Rosario Leone, Giuseppe De Santis, Roberto Rossellini, Diego Calcagno, Marcello Pagliero, Guglielmo Santangelo from a story by A. I. Benvenuti. Photographed by Rodolfo Lombardi, Ugo Lombardi. Music by Renzo Rossellini. 102 minutes.
With Elli Parvo (Paola), Massimo Girotti (Nando), Carlo Ninchi (Giovanni), Lia Corelli, Francesco Grandjacquet, Roswita Schmidt, Titi Rinaldi, Giovanna Scotto, Spartaco Conserva, Jucci Kellerman.
Finished by Marcello Pagliero in 1946.

1945: ROMA, CITTÀ APERTA – *Open City*
Directed by Roberto Rossellini. Production: Excelsa Film. Written by Sergio Amidei, Federico Fellini and Roberto Rossellini from a story by Sergio Amidei and Alberto Consiglio. Photographed by Ubaldo Arata. Décor by R. Megna. Edited by Eraldo Da Roma. Music by Renzo Rossellini. 100 minutes.
With Anna Magnani (Pina), Aldo Fabrizi (Don Pietro Pellegrini), Marcello Pagliero (Manfredi), Maria Michi (Marina), Harry Feist (Major Bergmann), Francesco Grandjacquet (Francesco), Giovanna Galletti (Ingrid), Vito Annichiarico (Marcello, the little boy), Carla Revere (Lauretta), Nando Bruno (Agostino), Carlo Sindici (police superintendent), Joop van Hulzen (Hartmann), Akos Tolnay (Austrian deserter), Eduardo Passarelli (policeman), Amalia Pelegrini (landlady), Alberto Tavazzi, C. Giudici.

1946: PAISÀ – *Paisan*
Directed and produced by Roberto Rossellini. Production: OFI, Foreign Film Production Inc., Capitani Film. Written by Federico Fellini and Roberto Rossellini, from stories by Victor Haines, Marcello Pagliero, Sergio Amidei, Federico Fellini, Roberto Rossellini, and in the Florence episode, Vasco Pratolini (uncredited); English dialogue by Annalena Limentani. Photographed by Otello Martelli. Edited by Eraldo Da Roma. Music by Renzo Rossellini. 124 minutes.
With – *I: Sicily*, Carmela Sazio (Carmela) Robert Van Loon (Robert), Carlo Pisacane (a peasant); *II: Naples*, Dots M. Johnson (the negro soldier), Alfonsino Pasca (the little boy); *III: Rome*, Maria Michi (Maria), Gar Moore (Gar); *IV: Florence*, Harriet White (Harriet), Renzo Avanzo (Massimo), Gigi Gori (a partisan); *V: Romagna*, Bill Tubbs (American priest); *VI: Po*, Dale Edmonds (Dale), Cigolani (the partisan), Benjamin Emanuel, Allan Dan, Leonard Parrish, Mats Carlson, Merlin Hugo, Anthony La Penna, Harold Wagner, Lorena Berg, Carlo Pisacane.

1947: GERMANIA, ANNO ZERO – *Germany, Year Zero*
Directed by Roberto Rossellini. Production: Tevere Film, Sadfilm. Written 'by Roberto Rossellini, Carlo Lizzani and Max Kolpet from a story by Roberto Rossellini. Photographed by Robert Juillard. Décor by Roberto Filippone. Edited by Eraldo Da Roma. Music by Renzo Rossellini. 75 minutes.
With Edmund Moeschke (Edmund), Franz Kruger (his father), Barbara Hintz (Eva), Werner Pittschau (Karlheinz), Erich Gühne (the professor), Alexandra Manys, Baby Reckvell, Ingetraut Hintze, Hans Sange, Hedi Blankner, the Count Treiberg, Karl Kauger.

1948: L'AMORE
Directed by Roberto Rossellini. Production: Tevere Film. 69 minutes.
I. (completed 1947) UNA VOCE UMANA: written by Roberto Rossellini from the one-act play, 'La voix humaine' by Jean Cocteau. Photographed by Robert Juillard. Décor by Christian Bérard. Music by Renzo Rossellini.
With Anna Magnani.
II. IL MIRACOLO – *The Miracle*: written by Tullio Pinelli and Roberto Rossellini from a story by Federico Fellini. Photographed by Aldo Tonti. Edited by Eraldo Da Roma. Music by Renzo Rossellini.
With Anna Magnani (Nanina), Federico Fellini (traveller).

1948: LA MACCHINA AMMAZZACATTIVI
Directed by Roberto Rossellini. Production: Universalia, Tevere Film (Roberto Rossellini). Written by Roberto Rossellini, Sergio Amidei, Giancarlo Vigorelli, Franco Brusati, Liana Ferri from a story by Eduardo De Filippo and Fabrizio Sarazani. Photographed by Tino Santoni and Enrico Betti Berutto. Edited by Luigi Rovere. Music by Renzo Rossellini. 80 minutes.
With Gennaro Pisano (Celestino), Marilyn Bufferd, Bill Tubbs and Helen Tubbs (American tourists), Giovanni Amato (the mayor), Piero Carloni, John Falletta, Clara Bindi, Camillo Buonnani, Giacomo Turia, Aldo Giuffrè, Aldo Nanni, Gajo Visconti, and the people of Majori, Amalfi and Atrani.

1949: STROMBOLI, TERRA DI DIO – *Stromboli*
Directed by Roberto Rossellini. Production: Be-Ro (Ingrid Bergman and Roberto Rossellini) for RKO. Written by Roberto Rossellini, Art Kohn, Sergio Amidei, Gianpaolo Callegari and Renzo Cesana from a story by Roberto Rossellini. Religious theme inspired by R. P. Felix Morlion. Photographed by Otello Martelli. Edited by Jolanda Benvenuti. Music by Renzo Rossellini. 107 minutes.
With Ingrid Bergman (Karin), Mario Vitale (Antonio), Renzo Cesana (the priest), Mario Sponza (the lighthouse keeper) and people of Stromboli.

1950: FRANCESCO, GIULLARE DI DIO
Directed by Roberto Rossellini. Production: Rizzoli Amato. Written by Roberto Rossellini, Federico Fellini, Felix Morlion and Antonio Lisandro from 'I fioretti di San Francesco'. Photographed by Otello Martelli. Décor by Virgilio Marchi. Edited by Jolanda Benvenuti. Music by Renzo Rossellini. 75 minutes.
With Aldo Fabrizi (Nicolaio), Arabella Lemaître (Chiara), Fra Nazario (Francesco) and non-professional actors.

1952: L'INVIDIA (Fifth episode of I SETTE PECCATI CAPITALI – *Les sept péchés capitaux* – *The Seven Deadly Sins*)
Directed by Roberto Rossellini. Production: Film Costellazione (Rome) and Franco London Film (Paris). Written by Roberto Rossellini, Diego Fabbri, Turi Vasile and Liana Ferri; story by Roberto Rossellini from 'La chatte' by Colette. Photographed by Enzo Serafin. Décor by Hugo Blaetter. Music by Yves Baudrier. 20 minutes.
With Andrée Debar (Camilla), Orfeo Tamburi (Orfeo), Nicola Ciarletta, Nino Franchina, R. M. De Angelis.
Other episodes directed by Yves Allégret, Claude Autant-Lara, Carlo-Rim, Jean Dreville, Eduardo De Filippo and Georges Lacombe.

1952: *Medico Condotto*
Directed by Giuliano Biagetti. Written by Roberto Rossellini and Antonio Pietrangeli. Supervised by Roberto Rossellini. Music by Renzo Rossellini.

1952: EUROPA '51
Directed by Roberto Rossellini. Production: Carlo Ponti and Dino De Laurentiis. Written by Sandro De Feo, Mario Pannunzio, Ivo Perilli, Brunello Rondi, Diego Fabbri, Antonio Pietrangeli and Roberto Rossellini from a story by Roberto Rossellini. Photographed by Aldo Tonti. Décor by Virgilio Marchi. Edited by Jolanda Benvenuti. Music by Renzo Rossellini. 110 minutes.
With Ingrid Bergman (Irene Girard), Alexander Knox (George Girard), Ettore Giannini (Andrea), Giulietta Masina ('Little Bird'), Teresa Pellati (Agnese, the prostitute), Sandro Franchina (Michele Girard), Bill Tubbs, Alfred Browne, Giancarlo Vigorelli, Bernardo Tafuri, Francesca Uberti, Carlo Hintermann, Mariemma Bardi, Marina Zanoli, Alessio Ruggeri, Giuseppe Chinnici, Mary Joham, Alberto Plebani, Vera Wicht, Gianna Damiani, Rossana Rory, Silvana Veronese.

1953: DOV'È LA LIBERTÀ?
Directed by Roberto Rossellini. Production: Carlo Ponti and Dino De Laurentiis, Golden Film. Written by Vitaliano Brancati, Antonio Pietrangeli, Ennio Flaiano and Vincenzo Talarico from a story by Roberto Rossellini. Photographed by Aldo Tonti and Tonino delli Colli. Décor by Virgilio Marchi. Edited by Jolanda Benvenuti. Music by Renzo Rossellini. 84 minutes.
With Totò (Salvatore Locajono), Vera Molnar (Agnese), Nyta Dover (Maria), Franca Faldini (Teresa), Leopoldo Trieste (Torquati), Giacomo Rondinella, Fortunato Misiano, Pasquale Misiano, Nino Misiano, Fernando Milani, Eugenio Orlandi, Augusta Mancini, Maria Bon Rosetti, Giacomo Gabrielli, Andrea Campagnoni, Thea Zubin, Ines Fiorentini, the dancers Ines Tarqas, Fred and Aronne.

1953: VIAGGIO IN ITALIA – *The Lonely Woman*
Directed by Roberto Rossellini. Production: Sveva-Junior-Italiafilm. Written by Roberto Rossellini and Vitaliano Brancati. Photographed by Enzo Serafin. Décor by Piero Filippone. Edited by Jolanda Benvenuti. Music by Renzo Rossellini. 75 minutes.
With Ingrid Bergman (Katherine Joyce), George Sanders (Alexander Joyce), Maria Mauban (Marie), Paul Muller (Paul Dupont), Leslie Daniels (Tony Burton), Natalia Ray (Natalie Burton), Anna Proclemer (the prostitute), Jackie Frost (Betty).

1953: INGRID BERGMAN (Third episode of SIAMO DONNE)
Directed by Roberto Rossellini. Production: Titanus-Film Costellazione. Written by Cesare Zavattini and Luigi Chiarini. Photographed by Otello Martelli. Edited by Jolanda Benvenuti. Music by Alessandro Cicognini. 20 minutes.
With Ingrid Bergman (herself), Albamarie Setaccioli (the neighbour).
Other episodes directed by Alfredo Guarini, Gianni Franciolini, Luigi Zampa, Luchino Visconti.

1953: Directed Giuseppe Verdi's opera 'Otello' at Teatro San Carlo (Naples).

1953: Directed 'Jeanne au bucher', play by Paul Claudel with music by Arthur Honegger, at Teatro San Carlo (Naples), La Scala (Milan), Opéra (Paris), Liceo (Barcelona), Stoll Theatre (London), etc.

1954: NAPOLI '43 (Fourth episode of AMORI DI MEZZO SECOLO)
Directed by Roberto Rossellini. Production: Excelsa, Roma Film. Written by Roberto Rossellini. Photographed in Ferraniacolor by Tonino Delli Colli. Décor by Mario Chiari. 15 minutes.
With Antonella Lualdi (Carla), Franco Interlenghi (Renato).
Other episodes directed by Glauco Pellegrini, Pietro Germi, Mario Chiari, Antonio Pietrangeli.

1954: GIOVANNA D'ARCO AL ROGO
Directed by Roberto Rossellini. Production: Produzione Cinematografiche Associate (Rome), Franco-London Film (Paris). Written by Roberto Rossellini, from the play by Paul Claudel. Photographed in Gevacolor by Gabor Pogany. Edited by Jolanda Benvenuti. Music by Arthur Honegger. 80 minutes.
With Ingrid Bergman (Giovanna), Tullio Carminati (Fra Domenico), Giacinto Prandelli, Saturno Meletti, Augusto Romani, Agnese Dubbini, Plinio Clabassi, Piero Di Palma, Aldo Terrosi, Silvio Santarelli, Gerardo Gaudioso, Anna Tarallo, Luigi Paolillo, the voices of Mariam Berazzini, Marcella Pobbe, Dina Cesca, Giovanni Avolanti.

1954: DIE ANGST – LA PAURA – *Non credo più all'amore – Fear*
Directed by Roberto Rossellini. Production: Aniene Film (Rome), Ariston Film (Munich). Written by Sergio Amidei and Franz Graf Treuberg from the story '*Angst*' by Stefan Zweig. Photographed by Carlo Carlini and Heinz Schnackertz. Edited by Jolanda Benvenuti and

Walter Boos. Music by Renzo Rossellini. 81 minutes.
With Ingrid Bergman (Irene Wagner), Mathias Wiedman (Albert Wagner), Renate Manhardt (Joanna Schultze), Kurt Kreuger (Enrico Stolz), Elise Aulinger (Marta), Edith Schultze-Westrum, Steffie Struck, Annelore Wied.

1954: *Orient Express*
Directed by Carlo Ludovico Bragaglia. Supervised by Roberto Rossellini.

1954: Directed 'La Figlia di Jorio', play by Gabriele D'Annunzio, with music by Ildebrando Pizzetti.

1958: L'INDIA VISTA DA ROSSELLINI
Directed and produced by Roberto Rossellini for RAI Radio-Televisione Italiana. 16 mm documentary in ten episodes (of 18–29 minutes each): 1) *India senza miti*; 2) *Bombay, la porta dell'India*; 3) *Architettura e costume di Bombay*; 4) *Varsova*; 5) *Verso il sud*; 6) *Le lagune del Malabar*; 7) *Il Kerala*; 8) *Hirakud, la diga sul fiume Mahadi*; 9) *Il Pandit Nehru*; 10) *Gli animali dell'India*. Broadcast January-March 1959, by RAI.

1958: *J'ai fait un beau voyage*
Directed by Jean Lhote. Production: RTF. With Roberto Rossellini interviewed by Etienne Lalou. French version of *L'India vista da Rossellini*, broadcast in ten episodes, January-August 1959, by RTF.

1958: INDIA
Directed by Roberto Rossellini. Production: Aniene Film (Rome) Union Générale Cinématographique (Paris). Written by Roberto Rossellini, Sonali Senroy das Gupta and Fereydoun Hoveyda from a story by Roberto Rossellini. Photographed in Gevacolor/Kodachrome by Aldo Tonti. Edited by Cesare Cavagna. Music by Giovanni Bross and Philippe Arthuys; Indian music adapted by Jean Daniélou. 90 minutes.
With non-professional actors.

1959: IL GENERALE DELLA ROVERE
Directed by Roberto Rossellini. Production: Zebra Film (Rome), SNE Gaumont (Paris). Written by Sergio Amidei, Diego Fabbri, Indro Montanelli and Roberto Rossellini from a story by Indro Montanelli. Photographed by Carlo Carlini. Décor by Piero Zuffi. Edited by Anna Maria Montanari. Music by Renzo Rossellini. 130 minutes.
With Vittorio De Sica (Bardone, alias Grimaldi), Hannes Messemer (Colonel Müller), Sandra Milo (Valeria), Giovanna Ralli (Olga), Anne Vernon (Chiara Fassio), Vittorio Caprioli (Banchelli), Ivo Garrani (Fabrizio).

1960: ERA NOTTE A ROMA
Directed by Roberto Rossellini. Production: International Golden Star (Genoa), Films Dismage (Paris). Written by Sergio Amidei, Diego Fabbri, Brunello Rondi and Roberto Rossellini from a story by Sergio Amidei. Photographed by Carlo Carlini. Décor by Flavio Mogherini. Costumes by Elio Costanzi. Edited by Roberto Cinquini. Music by Renzo Rossellini. 120 minutes.
With Leo Genn (Pemberton), Giovanna Ralli (Esperia), Sergei Bondarchuk (Fiodor), Hannes Messemer (von Kleist), Peter Baldwin (Bradley), Sergio Fantoni (Don Valerio), Enrico Maria Salerno (the doctor), Paolo Stoppa (Prince Antoniani), Renato Salvatore (Renato), Laura Betti (Virginia), Rosalba Neri (Erika), George Petrarca (Tarcisio), Giulio Calì, Carlo Reali, Leopoldo Valentini, Roberto Palombi.

1960: VIVA L'ITALIA
Directed by Roberto Rossellini. Production: Tempo, Galatea, Zebra Film. Written by Sergio Amidei, Diego Fabbri, Antonio Petrucci, Antonello Trombadori and Roberto Rossellini from a story by Sergio Amidei, Luigi Chiarini and Carlo Alianello. Photographed in Eastmancolor by Luciano Trasatti. Décor by Gepy Mariani. Costumes by Marcella de Marchis. Edited by Roberto Cinquini. Music by Renzo Rossellini. 138 minutes.
With Renzo Ricci (Giuseppe Garibaldi), Paolo Stoppa (Nino Bixio), Franco Interlenghi (Bandi), Giovanna Ralli (Rosa), Tina Louise (French journalist), Sergio Fantoni, Leonardo Botta, Carlo Gazzabini, Marco Mariani, Gérard Herter, Giovanni Petrucci, Pietro Bracciolini, Nando Angelmi, Vando Tress, Attilio Battegio, Luigi Borghese, Philippe Arthuys, Amedeo Buzzanca, Ignazio Balzamo, Bruno Scipione, Evar Maran, Amedeo Gerard, Armando Guarnieri, Giuseppe Lo Presti, Raimondo Croce, Vittorio Bottone, Renato Montalbano, Sveva Caracciolo D'Aguara.

1961: VANINA VANINI – *The Betrayer*
Directed by Roberto Rossellini. Production: Zebra Film (Rome), Orsay Film (Paris). Written by Roberto Rossellini, Franco Solinas, Antonello Trombadori, Diego Fabbri, Monique Lange and Jean Gruault from 'Chroniques Italiennes' and other works by Stendhal. Photographed in Eastmancolor by Luciano Trasatti. Costumes by Danilo Donati. Music by Renzo Rossellini. 125 minutes.
With Sandra Milo (Vanina Vanini), Laurent Terzieff (Pietro Missirilli), Martine Carol (Countess Vitteleschi), Paolo Stoppa (Prince Asdrubale Vanini), Isabelle Corey (Clelia), Nerio Bernardi (Cardinal Savelli), Olimpia Cavalli, Leonardo Botta, Antonio Pierfederici.

1961: TORINO NEI CENTI'ANNI
Directed by Roberto Rossellini. Production: PROA for
RAI Radio-Televisione Italiana. Written by Valentino
Orsini. Commentary by Vittorio Gorresio. Photographed
by Leopoldo Piccinelli, Mario Vulpiani and Mario
Volpi. 45 minutes.

1961: *Benito Mussolini*
Directed by Pasquale Prunas. Supervised by Roberto
Rossellini.

1961: Directed '*Un Sguardo dal ponte*', adapted from
Arthur Miller's 'A View from the Bridge' by Gerardo
Guerrieri with music by Renzo Rossellini, at the Rome
Opera.

1962: ANIMA NERA
Directed by Roberto Rossellini. Production: Documento
Film. Written by Roberto Rossellini from a play by
Giuseppe Patroni-Griffi. Photographed by Luciano
Trasatti. Décor by Elio Costanzi and Alfredo Freda.
Costumes by Marcella de Marchis. Edited by Daniele
Alabiso.
With Vittorio Gassman (Adriano), Nadja Tiller (Mim-
osa), Annette Stroyberg (Marcella), Eleonora Rossi-
Drago (Alessandra), Yvonne Sanson (Olga), Tony
Brown, Rina Braido, Giuliano Cocuzzoli, Daniela
Igliozzi, Chery Milion, Armando Suscipi.

1962: ILLIBATEZZA (Episode in ROGOPAG –
Laviamoci il cervello)
Directed and written by Roberto Rossellini. Production:
Arco Film. Photographed by Luciano Trasatti. Décor
by Flavio Mogherini. Music by Carlo Rusticelli.
With Rosanna Schiaffino (Anna Maria), Bruce Balaban
(Joe), Carlo Zappavigna (Carlo), Gianrico Tedeschi
(psychiatrist), Maria Pia Schiaffino.
Other episodes directed by Jean-Luc Godard, Pier
Paolo Pasolini and Ugo Gregoretti.

1962: Directed '*I Carabinieri*' a play by Beniamino
Joppolo at the Spoleto Festival. With Jean Gruault wrote
screenplay for the adaptation, *Les Carabiniers* (1963),
directed by Jean-Luc Godard.

1964: L'ETÀ DEL FERRO
Directed by Renzo Rossellini Jr. Production: 22
Dicembre, Istituto Luce. Written and supervised by
Roberto Rossellini. Photographed by Carlo Carlini.
Narrated by Giancarlo Sbragia. Documentary for
television consisting of five one-hour episodes.
With non-professional actors.

1966: LA PRISE DE POUVOIR PAR LOUIS XIV
Directed by Roberto Rossellini. Production: ORTF.
Written by Jean Gruault and Jean-Dominique de la
Rochefoucauld (uncredited) from a story by Philippe
Erlanger. Photographed in Eastmancolor by Georges
Leclerc. Décor by Maurice Valay. Costumes by Chris-
tiane Coste. Edited by Armand Ridel. Music arranged
by Betty Willemetz. 100 minutes.
With Jean-Marie Patte (Louis XIV), Raymond Jourdan
(Colbert), Silvagni (Mazarin), Katharine Renn (Anne of
Austria), Dominique Vincent (Madame du Plessis),
Pierre Barrat (Fouquet), Fernand Fabre (Le Tellier),
Françoise Ponty (Louise de la Vallière), Joëlle Langeois
(Marie-Thérèse), Jacqueline Corot (Mme Henriette),
Maurice Barrier (D'Artagnan), François Mirante
(Monsieur de Brienne), André Dumas (Père Joly), Pierre
Spadoni (Noni), Roger Guillo (pharmacist), Louis
Raymond (first doctor), Maurice Bourdon (second
doctor), Michel Ferre (Monsieur de Gesvres), Raymond
Pelissier (Pomponne), Michèle Marquais (Madame de
Motteville), Guy Pintat (head cook), Jean-Jacques Dubin
(Monsieur de Vardes), Georges Goubert (Monsieur de
Soyecourt), Pierre Pernet (King's brother), Claude Rio
(Vardes), Daniel Dubois (Lionne), Ginette Barbier
(Pierrette Dufour), Jean Obe (le Vau), Jacques Charby
(Le Vau's assistant), Micheline Muc (Mademoiselle de
Pons), Michel Debranne (the tailor), Rene Rabault
(Monsieur de Gramont), François Bernard (Archbishop),
Gerges Spanelly (Séguier), Jean Soustre (Monsieur de
Guiche), Axel Ganz (the ambassador), Jean-Jacques
Leconte (first chamberlain), Violette Marceau (Made-
moiselle de Chemerault), Paula Dehelly (Madame
d'Elboeuf), Jacques Preboist (first musketeer), Robert
Cransac (second musketeer), André Daguenet (skipper),
Françoise Deville (woman), Pierre Frag, Marc Fraiseau
and Jean Coste (sailors), Pierre Lepers (chaplain), Rita
Maiden (country-woman), Hélène Manesse (the naiad),
Jean-Claude Charnay (the messenger).

1967: IDEA DI UN'ISOLA
Directed by Roberto Rossellini. Production: Orizzonte
2000 (Roberto Rossellini). Photographed in colour
(Tecnostampa) by Mario Fioretti. One-hour documentary on Sicily for American television.

1967: LA LOTTA DELL'UOMO PER LA SUA
SOPRAVVIVENZA
Directed by Renzo Rossellini Jr. Production: Orizzonte
2000 (Roberto Rossellini) for Logos Film (Paris),
Romania Film (Bucharest), Copro Film (Cairo). Written
and supervised by Roberto Rossellini. Photographed in
colour (Tecnostampa) by Mario Fioretti. Décor by
D'Eugenio Saverio and Gepy Mariani. Costumes by

Marcella de Marchis. Music by Mario Nascimbene; theme song by Shirley Bassey. Documentary-feature for television in twelve one-hour episodes.
With non-professional actors.

1968: ATTI DEGLI APOSTOLI

Directed by Roberto Rossellini with the collaboration of Renzo Rossellini Jr. Production: Orizzonte 2000 for RAI (Rome), ORTF (Paris), TVE (Madrid) and Studio Hamburg (Hamburg), with collaboration of Les Films de Carthage. Written by Dominique de la Rochefoucauld, Vittorio Bonicelli, Luciano Scaffa and Roberto Rossellini from the Acts of the Apostles. Photographed in colour (Tecnostampa) by Mario Fioretti. Décor by Gepy Mariani and Carmelo Patrono. Costumes by Marcella de Marchis. Edited by Roberto Rossellini. Music by Mario Nascimbene. Theme song by Sonali Senroy. Feature film for television in five episodes, lasting 58 minutes, 58 minutes, 64 minutes, 64 minutes and 98 minutes.

With Edoardo Torricella (Paul), Jacques Dumur (Peter), Mohamed Ktari (Mark), Mohamed Kouka (John), Renzo Rossi (Zachariah), Ben Reayeb Moncef (Thomas), Beppi Mannaiuolo (Philip), Zignani Houcine (Stephen), Malo Brass (Aristarcus, the Greek scribe), Enrico Ostermann (Caiaphas), Daniele Dublino (Silas), Olimpia Carlisi (Lydia), Bradai Ridha (Matthew), Missoume Ridha (James the Greater), Zouiten (James the Less), Hedi Nouira (Andrew), Bouraoui (Bartholomew), Lydia Biondi (the pythoness), Dino Mele (Aquila), Maria Quasimodo (hostess in Corinth), Paul Muller (Greek sophist), Sergio Serafini (Roman christian), Gian Paolo Capovilla (Greek soldier in Neapolis).

1970: SOCRATE

Directed by Roberto Rossellini. Production: Orizzonte 2000 for RAI (Rome), ORTF (Paris), TVE (Madrid). Written by Jean-Dominique de la Rochefoucauld and Roberto Rossellini. Photographed in colour (Tecnostampa) by Jorge Herrero. Décor by Bernardo Ballester and Giusto Puri Purini. Costumes by Marcella de Marchis. Edited by Roberto Rossellini. Music by Mario Nascimbene. About 120 minutes.

With Jean Sylvère (Socrates), Anne Caprile (Xanthippe), Ricardo Palacios (Crito), Beppi Mannaiuolo (Apollodorus), Manuel Angel Egea (Cebetes), Julio Morales (Antisthenes), Jesús Fernández (Critobulus), Eduardo Puceiro (Simmias), José Renovales (Phaedo), Antonio Medina (Plato), Emilio Miguel Hernández (Meletus), Emilio Hernández Blanco (Hyperides), Gonzalo Tejel (Anytus), Antonio Requena (Hermes), Roberto Cruz (old man), Francisco Sanz (actor), Antonio Alfonso (Euthyphron), Juan Francisco Margallo (Critias), Román Ariznavarreta (Calicles), Francisco Catalá (Lysias), Adolfo Thous (Hippias), Jean-Dominique de la Rochefoucauld (Phaedrus), Bernardo Ballester (Theophrastus), César Bonet (priest), Jerzy Radlowski (juggler), Pedro G. Estecha (Phocion), Rafael de la Rosa (Thrasybulus), Simón Arriaga (man with hemlock), Iván Almagro (Hermogenes), Constant Rodríguez (Aristephus), Stefano Chorelli (Ephigenes), Luis Alonso (Aeschines), Jesús A. Gordon (Lamprocles), José Luis Ortega (Socrates' young son).

Bibliography

A. Texts by Rossellini

Dix ans de cinéma: Cahiers du Cinéma, 50, 52 and 55 (August-September, November 1955, January 1956). Reprinted in Italy as *Il mio dopoguerra*, Cinema Nuovo, 70, 72 and 77 (November, December 1955, February 1956). Also reprinted in *Roberto Rossellini* by Massimo Mida (second edition).

Lettera aperta all'On. Tupini: Schermi (October 1959). Also reprinted in Mida (op. cit.).

Censure et culture (open letter to Senator Renzo Helfer): Cinéma 61, n. 60 (October 1961).

Conversazione sulla cultura e sul cinema: Filmcritica, 131 (March 1963).

Cinema: nuove prospettive de conoscenza: Filmcritica, 135-136 (July-August 1963).

La ricerca di stile e di linguaggio e il rinnovamento del contenuto: Filmcritica, 167 (May-June 1966).

Comprimere nel tempo le esperienze di una vita, Cinema d'oggi, 3 (June 1968).

B. Synopses and Screenplays of Films by Rossellini

Roma, città aperta: L'Avant-Scène du Cinéma, 71.

Paisà: Sixth sketch: Bianco e Nero, October 1947. Reprinted in Filmcritica, 167 (May-June 1966). Also in *Roberto Rossellini* by Mario Verdone (in French).

Il Prigionero (sketch not filmed): Cinema Nuovo, 25 (April 1955); also reproduced in Verdone (op. cit.).

Il miracolo: Revue du Cinéma, 14 (June 1948).

Francesco, giullare di Dio: Inquadrature, September 1959.

Viaggio in Italia: Bianco e Nero, November 1953 (fragment); Filmcritica, 156-157 (April-May 1965) (complete).

India: As *Il donatore di terre*, Contemporaneo, January 1958; also in *Cinema Italiano del dopoguerra*, by Fabio Carpi, 1958. As *India*, in Verdone (op. cit.).

Era notte a Roma: (in series 'Dal soggetto al film') edited by Renzo Renzi, Cappelli, Bologna, 1961.

L'età del ferro: As *Il ferro*, Filmcritica, 139-140 (November-December 1963).

La prise de pouvoir par Louis XIV: Télè Sept Jours, October 1966.

Atti degli Apostoli: Cinema e Film, 9 (Summer 1969).

C. Interviews with Rossellini

Roberto Rossellini, Mario Verdone: *Coloquio sul neo-realismo*, Bianco e Nero, February 1952.

Maurice Schèrer, François Truffaut: *Entretien avec Roberto Rossellini*, Cahiers du Cinéma, 37 (July 1954).

André Bazin, Jean Renoir: *Cinéma et Télévision*, France-Observateur, 4 July 1957.

Jean Domarchi, Jean Douchet, Fereydoun Hoveyda: *Entretien avec Roberto Rossellini*, Cahiers du Cinéma, 133 (July 1962).

Fereydoun Hoveyda, Eric Rohmer: *Nouvel entretien avec Roberto Rossellini*, Cahiers du Cinéma, 145 (July 1963).

Adriano Aprà, Maurizio Ponzi: *Intervista con Roberto Rossellini*, Filmcritica, 156-157 (April-May 1965).

Lietta Tornabuoni: *Il cinema è morto*, L'Europeo, September 1966.

Jean Collet, Claude-Jean Philippe: *Entretien avec Roberto Rossellini*, Cahiers du Cinéma, 183 (October 1966).

Michele Mancin, Renato Tomasino, Lello Maiello: *Conversazione con Roberto Rossellini*, Filmcritica, 190 (August 1968).

D. Books about Rossellini

Patrice Hovald: *Roberto Rossellini*, Collection Encyclo-pédique du Cinéma, Club du Livre de Cinéma, 1958.

Massimo Mida: *Roberto Rossellini*, Guanda, Parma, 1953; Second Edition, 1961.

Mario Verdone: *Roberto Rossellini*, Cinéma d'aujourd'-hui, Editions Seghers, 1963.

E. About Roberto Rossellini: Magazine Articles

Maurice Schèrer: *Génie du christianisme*: Cahiers du Cinéma, 25 (July 1953).

François Truffaut: *Rossellini 55*, Arts, 19 January 1955.

Jacques Rivette: *Lettre sur Rossellini*, Cahiers du Cinéma, 46 (May 1955).

André Bazin: *Difesa di Rossellini*, Cinema Nuovo, 25 (August 1955). Reprinted in *Qu'est-ce que le cinéma?*, vol. IV (*Une esthétique de la réalité: le Néo-Réalisme*), Editions du Cerf, Paris, 1962.

Eric Rohmer: *Deux images de la solitude*, Cahiers du Cinéma, 59 (May 1956).

Jean-Luc Godard: *Un cinéaste, c'est aussi un missionnaire*, Arts, 1 April 1959. Reprinted in *Jean-Luc Godard par Jean-Luc Godard*, Editions Cahiers du Cinéma, Pierre Belfond, Paris, 1966.

Beniamino Joppolo: *La scelta assoluta di Roberto Rossellini*, Filmcritica, 96-97 (April-May 1960). Reprinted in the same magazine, 139-140 (November-December 1962).

Jean-André Fieschi: *Dov'è Rossellini?*, Cahiers du Cinéma, 131 (May 1962).

Adriano Aprà: *Le nouvel âge de Rossellini*, Cahiers du Cinéma, 169 (August 1965).

Maurizio Ponzi: *Due o tre cose su Roberto Rossellini*, Cinema e Film, 2 (Spring 1967) (this issue contains other very useful material by Gianfranco Albano, Luigi Faccini, Adriano Aprà, Luigi Martelli, Stefano Roncoroni, and Piero Spila.)

F. Other Sources quoted in this book

C.B., Cahiers du Cinéma, 67 (January 1957).

Bernard Eisenschitz: *L'Oeuvre de Roberto Rossellini*, L'Avant-Scène du Cinéma, 71.

Maurizio Ponzi: *Rome, ville ouverte*, L'Avant-Scène du Cinéma, 71.

R. M. de Angelis: *Rossellini romanziere*, Cinema 29-30 (December 1949).

Claude Beylie: Cahiers du Cinema, 122 (August 1961).

Adriano Aprà, Luigi Martelli: *Premesse sintagmatiche ad un'analisi di 'Viaggio in Italia'*, Cinema e Film, 2 (Spring 1967).

Marcel Oms: *Rossellini: du fascisme à la démocratie chrétienne*, Positif, 28 (April 1958).

Paul Mayersberg: *Vanina Vanini*, Movie, 6 (January 1963).

Louis XIV, la grande émission de Philippe Erlanger et Roberto Rossellini, Télé Sept Jours, October 1966.

Jean-Luc Godard: *India*, Cahiers du Cinéma, 96 (June 1959).

Postscript

I always try to remain impassive. I think that the surprising, extraordinary, moving thing about men is just that the great actions and achievements occur in the same way as the ordinary acts involved in living; it is with the same humility that I try to translate one into the other; there lies a source of dramatic interest.

Roberto Rossellini.

Each image is beautiful, not because it is beautiful in itself, like a shot from *Que viva Mexico*, but because it has the brilliance of truth, and because Rossellini sets out with the truth. Where others will only be arriving in maybe twenty years, he has already been.

Jean-Luc Godard.

Remember, Fabrizio! One cannot *live* without Rossellini!'

Gianni Amico/Bernardo Bertolucci
in Prima della rivoluzione